What Is It Worth?

ADVICE ON BUYING & SELLING ANTIQUES

by William & Georgie Farwell

CHARLES E. TUTTLE CO.
Rutland, Vermont

Representatives

For Continental Europe:
BOXERBOOKS, INC., *Zurich*

For the British Isles:
PRENTICE-HALL INTERNATIONAL, INC., *London*

For Australasia:
PAUL FLESCH & CO., PTY. LTD., *Melbourne*

For Canada:
M. G. HURTIG, LTD., *Edmonton*

Published by the Charles E. Tuttle Company, Inc.
of Rutland, Vermont & Tokyo, Japan
with editorial offices at
Suido 1-chome, 2-6, Bunkyo-ku, Tokyo

Library of Congress Catalog Card No. 73-75282
International Standard Book No. 0-8048 0980-1

First printing, 1973

Printed in Japan

Table of Contents

Foreword

One does not write a book in five minutes. But perhaps any book having to do generally with prices of antiques and art should, to be anywhere near accurate, be revised every five minutes. To one whose great interest is in market values, their constant increase is almost staggering. Vermont Royster, in the "Forewarning" to his book A Pride of Prejudices, *observes, "A small observation can be interesting but not the final proof of anything." We wish to think of this book as some small observations but not final proofs.*

While we take note of great collections and huge auction prices, we are especially interested in changes in the value of items in our own homes. These are not for the most part "collectors' items" but things we have acquired over the years by inheritance, gift, or purchase: articles of some merit and of continuing value.

Lists of prices in many categories of antiques show the increase in values over a period of years, and quote prices as of the 1968–69 period. At that time securities prices were high. But in late 1969 and in 1970 the prices of securities took a real nose dive. Not so with antiques. They continued to increase in value. Since that 1970 period the stock market has made a good recovery. At the same time the increase in values (and in actual sales) of antiques has been almost fantastic.

A study of our report of the James Campbell Lewis sale in July 1971 shows this. Our price quotes are mostly of what might be called high-priced collectors' items. We have in our files a complete list of all prices received. Lack of space forbids recording the whole list here. But the same fantastic rise in prices received held for all items of the more common variety.

Introduction

What is it worth? Ask an oldtime Yankee this question and his reply will be, "It's wuth what you can git for it." In a sense this is true. But it is not completely helpful in the selling or purchasing of antiques and art. Years ago the late Edwin LeFevre wrote a series of articles for the *Saturday Evening Post* on the subject of antiques. He stated that over the years two categories of antiques had had a steady and rather consistent increase in values: early silver and noteworthy books and manuscripts. This, generally speaking, is quite true but still subject somewhat to varying tastes, the state of the economy, and confidence (or lack of same) in other things of value such as gold, money, and securities.

There is no doubt that we are in the midst of a boom in antiques and art. It has been estimated that there are more than twenty thousand active antique dealers in the United States, more than double the number just one decade ago. It has also been estimated that Americans collectively spend twice as much money on antiques now as we did a few years ago. And the art market, as we shall see, has seen an almost unbelievable increase in volume of sales and prices paid for individual items.

One reason advanced for this terrific boom in sales of antiques and art has been the fear of inflation. We are not so sure about this. In some instances persons of great wealth have invested in art as a hedge against inflation. But we believe that the great volume of purchases of antiques and art have been made for other reasons. One important reason is the increase of disposable income by the great so-called middle class. Another reason is the awareness that purchases of art and antiques give a feeling of pleasure in owning beautiful things which at least do not depreciate in value and in a number of cases appreciate in value over the years. More and more people have been educated in appreciating what is of interest in design and style. And more and more people have learned that investment in modern furniture and up-to-the-minute motor cars is not an investment in continuing values but an investment that, dollars-and-cents-wise, depreciates at a very rapid rate.

Finally, let's admit it, all owners, buyers, sellers, and appraisers of antiques and art are interested in prices, or at least curious about them. For this reason we think it will be of interest to quote prices of some of the good, bad, or indifferent items.

1

Hammer & Gong

It was 1923. There had been a slight recession in securities prices in 1921. Generally things had improved. But there had not begun the great upward surge in prices which climaxed in 1929, only to be followed by a sickening slump leading to the Great Depression. On the stock market there was trading until Saturday noon, and the Dow-Jones industrials numbered twenty (versus thirty at the present time).

For five afternoons ending on Saturday, May 28, the entire stock of Mr. Benjamin Benguiat, trading as the Benguiat Corporation, was offered for sale at auction in the

American Art Galleries in New York City. The sale was "unrestricted"—that is to say, no items were "bid in" by representatives of the seller.

The Benguiat collection was made up entirely of unusually fine items assembled by a gentleman of extraordinary knowledge of what was really good. We have in our files a record of what was paid for each and every piece. It is impossible, of course, to list here all the items knocked down by the auctioneer's hammer. But in the list that follows we do give the actual amounts paid, mostly for furniture pieces listed in our catalogue. Opposite the prices paid we list what these items could be expected to bring in 1968. The 1968 figures are a consensus of opinion of experienced and knowledgeable dealers and private collectors, but not necessarily our own. From our many years of experience in appraisal work and in following sale and auction prices, our opinion would be that the 1968 price estimates are on the conservative side.

From 1923 to 1929 prices of antiques went up, along with securities and almost everything else. Perhaps the outstanding antique sale during this period was a Van Pelt Chippendale Highboy sold in 1928 for $44,000. This was an unusually high price, paid because the item was desired by two competing bidders with practically unlimited checking accounts.

Some of the items in the Benguiat sale were:

	1923 selling price	*Approx. 1968 value*
Maple-and-hickory Windsor armchair, horseshoe back and arms	$70.00	$200.00
Pine slant-front writing desk	95.00	1,000.00
Pair of unique carved and gilded forged-iron chandeliers	600.00	1,500.00
Set of 4 embroidered linen covers, English, 17th century	120.00	375.00
Needlepoint mahogany pole screen, English, early 18th century	100.00	250.00
American block front bureau, Goddard, *circa* 1750	375.00	4,000.00

	1923 selling price	*Approx. 1968 value*
Maple highboy, early 18th century	$300.00	$1,800.00
Carved mahogany lowboy, by William Savery	1,025.00	12,000.00
Carved maple highboy	325.00	3,000.00
Inlaid rosewood sofa table	190.00	750.00
Needlework mahogany bench	160.00	400.00
Welsh oak dresser	230.00	800.00
Washington carved and gilded mahogany mirror	330.00	1,200.00
Walnut inlaid chest on stand	260.00	800.00
Oyster-grained walnut chest on stand	270.00	1,500.00
Set of 6 carved walnut chairs	360.00	600.00
Decorated lacquer camp bed	200.00	800.00
Exceptionally fine pine settle	390.00	1,500.00

It is interesting to compare these increases in antique values with increases in the values of common stocks during the same period. If we compare the 1923 prices of five well-known stocks with their 1968 prices, taking into account splits and dividends, we find that American Telephone and Telegraph increased 276 percent; Corn Products, 890 percent; General Electric, 2,615 percent; U.S. Steel, 400 percent; and Texaco, 1,580 percent.

Many other stocks on the 1923 list of Dow-Jones Industrials, of course, have not done nearly as well—have lost in importance or been absorbed by other companies. In this category we think of American Locomotive, Baldwin Locomotive, Central Leather, or Studebaker. When comparing stock prices with antique prices, one must, of course, raise the important questions: Did you, years ago, buy the right antiques and the right stocks at the right prices? If you inherited them (as most owners of antiques and stocks do), have you hung onto the right stocks and the right antiques over the years? And there is always the question of needing—or at least liking—the stock dividends more than the pleasure of possessing antiques. We present the figures, not to prove anything, but just as an interesting comparison.

Looking at the prices of antiques and common stocks in general from 1925 to

1968, we find that antiques increased in value 263 percent and stocks 307 percent—a fair-sized increase in favor of stocks. In the period from 1950 to 1968, antiques increased 344 percent and stocks 377 percent, with the securities still running ahead. But in the short and recent period from 1960 to 1968, prices swung the other way. Antiques increased 196 percent, stocks 157 percent.

There have been, at times, wide swings. In the dismal depression year of 1932 antique prices held at 148 percent of 1925 prices while security prices slumped to 62 percent of 1925 prices.

Actually, over the whole 1925–68 period, there has not been much change in antique versus security prices. What *has* changed decidedly is the value of the dollar. A fine antique or a security sold in 1968 would bring a certain price, but what can be purchased with the money, compared with the buying power of the same amount of money in 1925? Fortunately, the resale value of antiques, like that of stocks, rises steadily ahead of the inflationary trends of the times.

2

To Be or Not To Be

Our notations on price changes in antiques and securities from the early twenties until now are given as a matter of interest, not to prove anything. Most of us are not Israel Sacks of antiques or Bernard Baruchs of the securities markets. Even if we were, most of us would lack the capital.

There is also, of course, the matter of tastes: what gives us real satisfaction and pleasure. And sometimes an injustice is done. There is a story, no doubt apocryphal, of the Boston lady who was asked where she and her friends bought their hats. "In Boston we *have* our hats," she answered.

Perhaps said hats might not be the last word in style, but we happen to know that many Boston ladies possess fine antiques, mostly "family," that make the spirits of antique lovers rise and that will be of great value and much cherished long after hats for females have changed in style or even disappeared altogether.

After the 1929 crash there were those in the securities markets who had made quick fortunes by short sales, and others who found themselves wiped out and ready to jump out a window. For those who were wiped out, the principal reason was credit —margin accounts with insufficient funds to meet margin calls, and their accounts consequently sold out fast. The real wealth of the country was in the hands of those who owned their stocks and bonds outright. It was probably annoying, but that was the situation. Wealthy folks were in a position to sit back and wait for things to improve. And some of the great wealth of the country was in a position to make purchases in an attempt to stabilize things.

By 1929 antiques had increased in price, and in the following depression they went down. But the rise and fall in antique values was less dramatic than in other businesses. Most dealers, for instance, owned their stocks of objects outright, and comparatively few were forced to sell at sickening depression prices. There never was any chance to buy antiques on margin, and antiques were never considered good collateral for loans. We remember (with a smile) one dealer who, as the depression lengthened, was short of capital and went to a crusty old banker for a loan. He was greeted with: "Ridiculous. Antiques have only sentimental value. No good for collateral." We happened to know something about that dealer's stock and what it turned out to be worth. And we also happened to know what a shellacking that same banker received on a loan he considered well collateralized.

3

Our Cherished Possessions

Rarely do any of us have in our homes anything in the way of antiques that might be called collectors' items or rare specimens. But we do have things of interest, and we are curious about changes in their monetary value over a period of years. Our own judgment may be warped by sentiment or other emotions. We say, "That's a good Hepplewhite stand. Belonged to great Aunt Harriet. She was a miserable old so-and-so. Wouldn't give you a pleasant smile. But anyway I have the stand and it's worth something." Or we may say, "That etched flip glass was dear Grandma Lovelace's. It probably isn't worth as much as we think it is. But we wouldn't part with it for anything."

In this chapter we list, in very limited numbers, the value or probable sale prices of items in different categories both in about 1950 and at the present time. This account of changes in values is derived from old and present pricing books, from friends who are specialists in the various sales records in general, and, in a number of instances, from actual sales in cases where estates have been liquidated under our direction.

We hasten to state that our figures are not "right on the dot." Any number of arguments could be brought to question individual figures. But we do know that the figures are correct in showing a trend—a trend that has been almost unbelievably upward. If an antique dealer with ordinary judgment of what was good (and in some cases perhaps not so good) had had in 1950 the capital and storage facilities to acquire a large collection of antiques, held them until the present year, and then sold them without too much difficulty, the profit, after allowing for interest on the money invested and cost of storage, would be very handsome indeed.

	1950 prices	*Present prices*
BELLEEK WARE		
Bowl, 3″ high	$12.00	$16.00
Cake plate	9.50	20.00
Creamer, 4½″, Bacchus heads & grapes	8.00	22.00
Cup & saucer	10.00	15.00
Sugar bowl, covered, basket weave & shamrocks	8.50	20.00
Vase (bud), apple blossoms	5.50	12.75
BELLS		
Chanticleer handle, small	5.00	12.00
School, wooden handle, small	3.25	12.50
School, wooden handle, large	5.25	18.50
Sleigh, string, iron	7.50	22.50
Sleigh, string, brass	12.50	45.00
BENNINGTON		
Bed pan	5.00	12.75
Bowl, octagonal, 13½″	15.00	30.00
Hound, 10″ high, on base	37.50	98.50
Pie plate, 10½″ × 1½″	3.50	16.00

Pitcher, boar & stag, 2 qt., pewter lid	$22.50	$75.00
Pitcher, hound handle, eagle under snout, birds & animals	25.00	125.00
Pudding mold	4.00	14.00

BISQUE

Match holder, "Happy Hooligan"	5.00	12.50

BRASS

Basket, French handle	7.00	12.00
Boot jack, "Naughty Nelly"	7.00	9.50
Box, hammered brass, 7″×7″	4.75	7.50
Bucket, 18″, good condition	15.00	30.00
Candle holder, saucer type	6.00	8.50
Candlesticks, pair, Chinese dragon	12.50	18.00
Dipper, old, 6″ diameter	7.50	15.00
Inkwell with tray, English	10.00	29.50
Powder horn, American Eagle, small	7.50	27.50

BUTTER MOLDS

Pineapple design, large	3.00	6.75
Round, leaf design	3.00	6.00
Round, one-pound size	5.50	10.00

CALENDAR PLATES

1909, small flowers & scenes	3.00	6.50
1915, "Panama Canal"	3.00	8.00

	1950 prices	*Present prices*
1918, 4 birds in border, 2 deer in center	$3.00	$7.50
1919, flags of 4 countries	3.50	8.25
1921, blue birds & pink flowers	3.00	6.50

CHINA

Blue Canton:		
Bouillon cup & saucer, covered	5.00	25.00
Bowl, cut corner, 10″ diam.	50.00	150.00
Cup & saucer, plain handle	3.00	25.00
Cup & saucer, wishbone handle	10.00	25.00
Drum tea set	25.00	50.00
Hot water dish	20.00	60.00
Mug	25.00	50.00
Pitcher	25.00	75.00
Platter, octagonal	5.00	45.00
Teapot, squat, on stand	50.00	150.00
Capo-di-Monti:		
Box, 4½″ × 3½″, "children"	24.50	65.50
Cup & saucer	21.50	45.00
Figurines, pair, 9¾″, child	120.00	215.00
Tankard, open, 8½″, elephant handle	100.00	195.00
Vases, pair, 15″, square base	350.00	465.00

Carlsbad:		
Fish set, 13 pieces	$75.00	$125.00
Chalkware:		
Rabbit, Pennsylvania Dutch	12.00	28.00
Squirrel, Pensylvania Dutch	13.50	35.00
Chelsea:		
Creamer, raised lustre flowers	7.50	18.00
Cup & saucer, purple grapes	4.50	20.00
Sauce dish, purple grapes	4.50	20.00
Sauce dish, purple grapes	2.00	8.75
Teapot, lustre grapes	21.00	65.00
China mugs:		
"A Brother's Gift," Staffordshire	7.50	20.00
"A Present for Sarah," early, 2″	7.50	20.00
"For Eliza," blue & black	7.50	15.00
"Mary," 2½″, blue & white	7.00	15.00
"Martha," seesaw & children	7.50	16.50
Cloissonne:		
Bird, 5½″	12.50	30.00
Bowl, 3″	6.50	13.50
Box, 3½″ × 4″, floral	6.00	12.75
Incense burner, 9¼″	32.50	65.00
Inkwell, covered	8.50	20.00
Jardinere & stand	50.00	95.00
Plate, 7″, blue	8.50	16.00
Vase, 9″, blue, butterflies	12.00	32.50
Dresden:		
Bowl, low, oval, late	10.00	30.00
Candelabra, 2-branch, pair	235.00	450.00
Cup & saucer, demitasse	12.00	35.00

	1950 prices	Present prices
Cup & saucer from chocolate set	$12.50	$32.50
Figurine, frog musicians	89.50	195.00
Tea set, pot, sugar & creamer	45.00	125.00
Haviland-Limoges:		
Butter dish, covered	7.50	18.50
Butter pat plate	1.00	2.75
Chocolate pot	7.50	22.50
Coffee service, 3-piece	25.00	60.00
Cup & saucer (tea), rose decoration	5.00	10.00
Dinner set, 80 pieces	100.00	225.00
Dinner set for 12, "Wedding Ring"	165.00	280.00
Dresser set, 5-piece	16.50	40.00
Oyster plates, set of 6	15.00	40.00
Perfume bottle, green & gold	3.00	7.50
Plate, 8½", hand-painted	5.00	12.50
Platter, 10" × 14½"	6.50	16.00
Tea set for 8, "Wedding Ring"	60.00	125.00
Tureen, oval	8.00	25.00
Leeds:		
Cup & saucer, handleless	15.00	30.00
Pepper pot	15.00	26.50
Platter, open edge	30.00	50.00

CLOCKS

Anniversary, 8" high, German	75.00	95.00

Banjo, Gilbert, 8-day	$30.00	$75.00
Calendar, 8-day	35.00	60.00
Eli Terry, pillar & scroll	150.00	475.00
French Gothic	30.00	55.00
Grandfather, cherry, good running condition	395.00	1,150.00
Seth Thomas, brass ship's clock	30.00	72.50
Steeple, mahogany, 8-day	35.00	65.00

COPPER

Boiler	10.00	25.00
Chafing dish	25.00	35.00
Coffee pot, good condition	9.50	16.50
Dow pot, Dutch, large	75.00	95.00
Pail, 16″	15.00	32.50
Pan, 13″×9″ deep	18.00	40.00
Teakettle, Norwegian	19.50	35.00
Weather vane, cow	22.00	195.00

COPPER LUSTRE

Bowl, 5½″, covered	24.00	49.50
Bowl, waste, blue	25.00	38.50
Cup & saucer, scalloped edge	15.00	34.50
Mug, 3½″, plain	8.50	22.50
Mug, shaving	18.50	30.00
Pitcher, 3″, sanded band	7.50	21.50
Salt, open, footed	10.50	18.50
Toby jug	24.50	80.00
Pitcher, blue band, 5¼″, lustre design	21.50	47.50

	1950 prices	Present prices
FURNITURE		
Beds:		
Cannon ball, refinished	$32.50	$72.50
Jenny Lind, full-size	21.50	100.00
Chairs:		
Captain's, roll-back type	35.00	75.00
Curly maple, set of 8 good	250.00	375.00
Hitchcock, good	37.50	55.00
Queen Anne, *circa* 1730, rough	38.50	200.00
Victorian Gentleman's, grape carving	100.00	195.00
Victorian Lady's, finger carved	65.00	165.00
Windsor, bow back, early	37.50	65.00
Windsor, comb back rocker	27.50	79.50
Chests:		
Cherry, refinished	95.00	180.00
Chippendale style, curly maple	225.00	575.00
Commode, pine, lift top	37.50	75.00
Highboy, Queen Anne, early, rough	540.00	1,250.00
Pine blanket chest, one long drawer	45.00	95.00
Corner Cupboards:		
Cherry, one-drawer, 2 glass doors on top, 2 solid doors below	110.00	220.00
Cherry, Chippendale influence, good	600.00	950.00

Pennsylvania Dutch jelly cupboard, rough	$28.00	$65.00
Pine, 2 panelled doors, center drawer, rough	40.00	87.50
Cradles:		
Pine, 43″ rockers, good	20.00	42.00
Walnut, 45″ rockers, original condition	15.00	28.50
Desks:		
Cherry, slat front, Chippendale	400.00	750.00
Curly maple, slant top, good	300.00	800.00
Schoolmaster's, walnut, rough	27.50	52.50
Victorian lady's	35.00	75.00
Dry sinks:		
Pine	35.00	85.00
Poplar high back	85.00	195.00
Frames:		
Gold leaf	5.00	15.00
Walnut, criss-cross corners	3.00	10.50
Walnut, oval, pair	7.50	37.50
Love seats:		
Victorian, walnut, large & good	75.00	275.00
Walnut, finger carved, fine	40.00	175.00
Walnut, late Victorian	30.00	60.00
Mirrors:		
Brass, standing for dressing table	14.00	35.00
Chippendale, inlaid mahogany gilt eagle	72.50	180.00

	1950 prices	*Present prices*
Mahogany, 2-section, painting in top	$21.00	$45.00
O.G., 28″×42″, good	17.50	35.00
Secretaries:		
Empire, 6′ high, veneer	125.00	225.00
Hepplewhite, mahogany, Tambour doors	300.00	600.00
Sheraton, inlaid, small reeded legs	295.00	475.00
Settees:		
Long spindle back, original	35.00	75.00
Small spindle back, pine	25.00	85.00
Settles:		
Pennsylvania Dutch, Hitchcock original	100.00	300.00
Sideboards:		
Empire, mahogany, cherry top & ends	145.00	300.0
Hepplewhite, inlaid, good condition	340.00	700.00
Sheraton, mahogany, 6 legs	700.00	800.00
Spice boxes:		
Walnut 6-drawer, as found	12.00	25.00
Walnut 8-drawer, refinished	18.00	40.00
Spinning wheels:		
Standard type, complete	20.00	45.00
Stands:		
Candle, tripod base, maple	20.00	65.00

Cherry 2-drawer, drop leaf, good	$45.00	$150.00
Cherry, 2 curly maple drawers	55.00	125.00
Cherry one-drawer, refinished, drop leaf	35.00	95.00
Mahogany 2-drawer, drop leaf, pedestal	40.00	120.00
Mahogany Duncan Phyfe card table, turned reeded legs	150.00	295.00
Maple 2-drawer, drop leaf	35.00	110.00
Maple one-drawer, turned legs	15.00	45.00

Tables:

Banquet, cherry, drop leaf	500.00	700.00
Banquet, mahogany, Hepplewhite, 3-section	500.00	1,000.00
Card table, cherry	85.00	225.00
Chippendale card table, walnut	250.00	450.00
French Marquetry, mahogany	50.00	130.00
Pembroke cherry, good original	90.00	185.00
Pembroke cherry, Hepplewhite	82.50	180.00
Queen Anne tea table, maple	400.00	1,200.00
Rope leg cherry drop leaf	79.00	270.00
Tilt top, maple, Serpentine edge	95.00	280.00
Tilt top, 17½" diameter	55.00	175.00
Tavern, small	65.00	150.00
Walnut, marble, turtle top	45.00	95.00

	1950 prices	*Present prices*
Wagon seat:		
Windsor type	$30.00	$60.00
What nots:		
Soft wood, corner, 5-shelf	25.00	70.00
Walnut, corner, bottom cupboard	45.00	120.00
Walnut, 5-shelf	50.00	135.00

GAUDY DUTCH WARE

"Carnation":		
Cup and saucer	48.50	225.00
Plate, 8¼″	60.00	300.00
Plate, 9¾″	75.00	325.00
"Dove":		
Cup and saucer	60.00	235.00
Plate, 6-3/8″, flat, sectional border	62.50	300.00
"Single Rose":		
Cup and saucer	37.50	220.00
Plate, 8″	50.00	375.00

GAUDY WELSH WARE

"Oyster" cup & saucer	9.50	30.00
"Shanghai" creamer	14.50	36.50
"Strawberry" creamer	21.50	42.00
"Tulip" cup & saucer	10.00	40.00
"Wagon wheel" plate, 8″	12.00	36.00

GAUDY IRONSTONE WARE

Cup & saucer, blackberry decoration	$12.00	$25.00
Pitcher, 5″	24.00	48.00
Plate, soup	8.00	18.50

GLASS

Amberina glass:		
Bowls, large	37.50	85.00–125.00
Butter dish	35.00	135.00
Celery vases	17.50	75.00–115.00
Creamer, minature	18.00	70.00
Decanter, cut stopper	35.00	125.00
Salt shaker, pewter top	7.00	27.00
Tumbler	10.00	30.00–35.00
Apothecary bottles:		
Various	3.00–5.00	5.00–15.00
Baccarat glass:		
Decanters (pair) with 12 wines	125.00	220.00
Inkwell	35.00	60.00
Paperweight (date 1847)	275.00	400.00 (up)
Barber bottles:		
Clear & colored, some Bohemian, some milk glass, various sizes and shapes	5.00–10.00	30.00–60.00
Bohemian glass:		
Cordial, vintage pattern	5.00	8.00
Decanter, tall & narrow	20.00	45.00

	1950 prices	Present prices
Finger bowl, vintage pattern	$10.00	$20.00
Goblet, vintage pattern	8.00	20.00
Tumbler, vintage pattern	7.00	15.00
Wine glass, vintage pattern	7.00	10.00
Bristol glass:		
Dresser set, 3 pieces	25.00	45.00
Fairy lamp, blue, swirled	20.00	75.00
Plaque, wall	4.00	12.00
Plate	10.00	25.00
Vase, enamel decoration	15.00	30.00
Vase, jack-in-the-pulpit	10.00	22.50
Burmese glass:		
Candlestick, diamond quilted	20.00	175.00
Creamer, 5½″ high	25.00	200.00
Finger bowl, scalloped	15.00	160.00
Shaker, sugar, pewter top	12.00	195.00
Sugar bowl, 5½″, crimped top	20.00	275.00
Vase, 12″	30.00	465.00
Cameo glass:		
Bowl, 4½″ diam., signed "Gallo"	15.00	125.00
Bowl, punch, signed "Thos. Webb & Sons"	300.00	1,200.00
Plate, 7½″, scalloped	12.00	75.00

Vase, 10½″, signed "Val St. Lambert"	$32.00	$110.00
Vase, 12½″, signed "Honesdale"	25.00	95.00
Carnival glass:		
Butter dish, amber	2.75	9.00
Epergne, purple to green	27.50	28.50
Plate, 9½″, bluish	3.50	9.00
Vase, 11½″, scalloped top	3.75	15.00
Cranberry glass:		
Bowl, 5½″, footed	17.50	35.00
Cordial set, tray, decanter & 8 cordials	32.50	72.50
Cruet, clear handle	16.50	40.00
Pitcher, ruffled top	35.00	48.50
Tumbler, opalescent	5.00	15.00
Vase, 4″, applied clear handle	12.00	21.50
Decanters:		
Black raised, pair, original stopper	12.00	25.00
Bohemian red, pointed stopper, vintage pattern	20.00	46.50
Bohemian red, pair, traces of gold decoration	32.50	55.00
Deep star, pair, channel cut	20.00	42.00
Early blown, 3 rings	12.00	28.50
Waffle & thumbprint, old	10.00	22.00
End-of-day glass:		
Perfume bottle, brass top, small	7.50	24.00

	1950 prices	*Present prices*
Pitcher, 9½″	$30.00	$72.50
Sugar shaker, pink	8.50	19.50
Vase, 8″	10.00	52.50
Fairy lamps:		
Burmese	20.00	300.00
"Clarkes"	20.00	40.00
Mary Gregory glass:		
Basket, fruit, amethyst	25.00	67.00
Barber bottle, amethyst	8.50	42.00
Barber bottle, cobalt blue	12.50	45.00
Barber bottle, green	10.00	42.00
Box, 4″, hinged	20.00	59.50
Box, jewel, blue & white	22.50	72.00
Butter dish, covered	13.50	89.50
Decanter, blown, blue	35.00	48.50
Pitcher, cranberry	25.00	87.50
Sugar shaker	6.50	36.50
Tumbler, clear	6.50	21.00
Vases, pair, 8″, green	25.00	80.00
Mercury glass:		
Lamps, pair, 10″ high	50.00	62.50
Vase, 12″ high	3.25	10.00
Vases, pair, 11½″, decorated	7.00	15.00
Milk glass:		
Blackberry creamer	10.00	22.50
Bowl, lacy, floral lattice	16.00	44.50
Compote, flint, early	26.50	48.00
Plates, gothic, 7¼″	4.50	9.00

Plates, wicket, 7½″	$6.00	$10.75
Vase, 9½″	3.50	9.00

Nailsea:

Fair lamp, frosted, 5½″	45.00	100.00
Globe for Gone with Wind lamp	50.00	115.00
Witch ball, large, pink & white	25.00	39.50

Peachblow:

Celery vase, Wheeling	30.00	285.00
Creamer, 5½″, applied handle	32.50	245.00
Rose bowl, New England	15.00	195.00
Salt, glossy, Wheeling	10.00	95.00
Tumbler, New England	9.50	225.00

Satin glass:

Berry bowl	12.50	69.50
Bowl, in silver frame	50.00	120.00
Box	35.00	80.00
Box, 7½″, white with pink	29.50	80.00
Cookie jar, silver bail	11.50	60.00
Cracker jar, silver lid	15.00	75.00
Perfume bottles	20–30.00	40–55.00
Pickle castor, blue, diamond quilted, in silver frame	35.00	125.00
Pitcher, pink, diamond quilted	40.00	185.00
Sugar shaker, melon shaped	9.00	40.00
Tumbler, pink, quilted	8.50	65.00
Tumbler, pink, diamond quilted	10.00	65.00
Vases, various	35–45.00	150–250.00

	1950 prices	Present prices
Tiffany glass:		
Candlesticks, pair	$40.00	$100.00
Champagne, hollow stem	10.00	65.00
Decanter	20.00	175.00
Jelly compote	45.00	175.00
Plate	15.00	90.00
Rummer	35.00	120.00
Urn, small	10.00	60.00
Vases, various	25–35.00	75–125.00
Venetian glass:		
Compote, high, blue	30.00	60.00
Cup & saucer, punch, green	6.50	20.00
Rummer, 8½″, ruby	30.00	58.50
Vase, 9½″, applied leaves	35.00	67.50
Waterford glass:		
Decanter, whiskey	22.50	67.50
Lustres, pair, 12½″	175.00	250.00
Tumbler, cut	4.50	12.50
Vases, pair, cut, heavy	50.00	89.60

GLASS, DEEP CUT

Bowl, mayonnaise, with stand	25.00	35.00
Bowl, punch, with separate base	150.00	225.00
Bowl, round	15.00	25.00
Cruets, matching pair	20.00	35.00

Dish, butter, covered	$35.00	$80.00
Dish, serving, oval, marked "Hawkes"	15.00	35.00
Knife rest	5.00	7.50
Pitcher, water	15.00	35.00
Sugar & creamer	15.00	27.50

GLASS, PRESSED

Argus goblet	5.50	12.00
Ashburton wine	6.00	11.00
Baltimore Pear berry bowl	8.00	12.00
Banded Buckle butter dish	7.50	14.00
Bellflower champagne	13.50	22.50
Bull's Eye tumbler	6.75	21.50
Carmel Slag goblet	20.00	65.00
Comet butter dish, covered, Washington knob	50.00	99.50
Daisy & Button butter dish in apple green	10.00	30.00
Diamond Thumbprint goblet, rare	32.50	135.00
Feather water pitcher	6.50	10.00
Garfield Drape goblet	3.75	7.75
Hamilton goblet	6.00	10.75
Horn of Plenty goblet	12.00	20.00
Horseshoe goblet, plain stem	3.25	8.75
Inverted Fern sugar bowl	12.00	28.50
Lincoln Drape goblet	5.00	15.00
Purple Slag small square dish	5.00	20.00

	1950 prices	*Present prices*
IRON		
Andirons, 30″, pair	$9.00	$24.00
Apple peeler, early	4.00	6.00
Boot jack, Beetle	3.50	7.50
Boot scraper	6.00	7.00
Coffee mill	7.50	15.00
Tongs	4.50	12.00
Trivets, good	2.50	10.00
Doorstops:		
Bulldog	3.75	10.00
Cat	6.00	12.50
Fluting Iron	4.00	4.75
Hitching Post Horse's Head	50.00	75.00
Kettle, footed	3.50	6.00
Little Red Riding Hood, pair	5.50	10.00
IRONSTONE		
Bowl, Meakin, 8″ square	4.00	7.50
Butter dish, covered	8.00	16.00
Cake plate, square	5.00	10.00
Platter, 14½″, "Lily of the Valley"	8.00	16.50
Soup tureen, "Wheat," large, with tray & ladle	35.00	50.00
JASPERWARE (Wedgwood)		
Bowl, light blue, 5⅛″	11.50	35.00
Bowl, light green, 7″	20.00	49.50

Box, green covered, heart shaped	$9.50	$32.50
Candlesticks, royal blue, 5¼″ high	30.00	57.50
Cookie jar, dark blue, silver cover	30.00	57.50
Creamer, 2″ high	9.00	29.50
Cup & saucer, early, blue	35.00	57.50
Jardinere, green, classic	28.50	55.00
Pitcher, 5½″, green, flowers and figures	27.50	50.00

LAMPS

Astral, 26″ prisms	60.00	125.00
Flint glass, whale oil, pattern bowl	10.00	25.00
Gone with the Wind, pink, red roses	35.00	85.00
Student lamp, 7″, double	95.00	175.00
Sweetheart lamp, green bowl	6.50	15.00
Tiffany, bronze & favrille glass (signed)	125.00	250.00

LANTERNS

Auto oil lamp, 14½″, brass	18.50	35.00
Captain ship lantern, copper reflector	22.50	50.00
Carriage lamps, pair, 15″	25.00	75.00
Paul Revere, large	6.00	27.50
Policeman's hand lantern, pair	5.00	11.50

	1950 prices	*Present prices*
Street post lantern	$40.00	$90.00

LIVERPOOL POTTERY

Jug, 4½″, obverse "Decator"	65.00	90.00
Jug, 8″, obverse "Madison"	70.00	200.00
Jug, 9½″, obverse "Washington" & eagles	65.00	320.00

LOWESTOFT

Bowl, 5½″	37.50	150.00
Cup & saucer, handleless	15.00	37.50
Teapot, 5¼″, 18th century	40.00	85.00

MAJOLICA

Asparagus dish & platter	12.00	27.00
Bread plate, 11″	13.50	21.00
Deep dish, 9″, leaf shaped	7.50	15.00
Mug, 3½″, lavender flowers	4.50	9.00
Pickle leaf, 7½″	5.00	9.50
Pitcher, 4¼″, blackberries	5.00	11.50
Plate, 9½″, green on white	6.00	11.50
Plate, 9½″, footed, green on white	11.00	20.00

MEISSEN, ONION

Bowl, 5¾″	15.00	18.50
Pitcher	18.50	24.50

Platter, 17″	$17.00	$29.50
Plate, 8½″	5.75	11.00
Plate with hot water jacket	15.00	18.50
Sugar bowl & creamer	35.00	49.50

MOCHA

Cup, 4½″ diam.	20.00	45.00
Muffineer, "Seaweed"	15.00	27.50
Mug, 6″, "Twig"	30.00	55.00

PARIAN

Bust of Dickens	8.00	32.50
Hand holding vase, urn shaped	21.50	32.00
Pitcher, 9″	7.50	35.00
Trinket box	12.50	18.50
Vase, cornucopia, 8″	15.00	22.50
Vase, 2 handles, 8¼″	16.00	32.00

PEWTER

Basin, unmarked, 10¼″	12.00	48.00
Basin, Boardman, 8″	25.00	75.p0
Bowl, 8″	20.00	75.00
Candlestick, Dunham, 6″	17.00	48.00
Candlestick, Gleason, saucer type	15.00	50.00
Coffee pot, J. Danforth, 11″	15.00	75.00
Coffee pot, 9″, dome top, Trask	20.00	65.00
Coffee pot, Morey & Sons	10.00	45.00
Charger, English, 20″	30.00	75.00

	1950 prices	Present prices
Flagon, unmarked	$25.00	$75.00
Pitcher, unmarked (covered)	25.00	65.00
Plate, unmarked, 8″	5.00	14.00
Plate, Wm. Danforth, 8″	18.00	65.00
Porringer, crown handle, 5¼″	20.00	60.00
Teapot, R. Gleason, 7″	16.00	65.00

QUIMPER

Bowl, 10¼″, pink & blue	8.00	12.50
Butter tub, covered, 4½″	4.75	12.50
Cup & saucer, square	5.50	10.00
Pitcher, water	11.50	22.50
Plate, 8″	3.75	9.75
Teapot, blue, red & white	10.00	22.50

ROOKWOOD

Jardinere, 8″ diameter	9.50	38.50
Pitcher, 10″	10.00	65.00
Pitcher vase, dated 1901	5.50	35.00
Vase, 8½″	14.50	46.50

ROYAL BAYREUTH

Box, covered	5.00	12.50
Box, large, tapestry portrait	18.50	40.00
Candle holder, Cape Cod	6.50	20.00

Dish, covered, tomato	$6.50	$20.00
Dish, covered, tomato (small)	3.75	12.00
Hat pin holder, tapestry	7.50	37.50
Pitcher, rose tapestry	7.50	48.50
Plate, 7″, leaf, handles	4.00	18.00

ROYAL COPENHAGEN

Compote, marked	19.50	45.00
Cruet, original stopper, blue & white	18.00	35.00
Cup & saucer	8.50	20.00
Dish, oval, blue & white	6.00	14.00
Plate, 7½″, Christmas	12.00	18.00
Plate, soup, blue & white	5.00	8.50
Teapot	10.00	37.50

ROYAL DOULTON

Compote	9.50	21.50
Cup & saucer	6.00	10.00
Jardiniere, 8″ diameter	7.50	16.50
Pitcher, 9½″, tan with leaf	13.50	21.50
Plate, 10″, pink willow	3.00	7.50
Plate, 9″, Dickens character	6.50	13.00
Vase, small iris decoration	10.00	15.00

ROYAL WORCESTER

Bowl, Dr. Wall period	22.50	75.00
Cup & saucer, pink flower	7.00	19.50
Cup & saucer, demitasse	10.00	12.75
Plate, 8¼″, floral scene	11.00	18.50

	1950 prices	*Present prices*
SATSUMA		
Cake plate, 1½″, flower border	$6.50	$18.00
Cup & saucer, 2-handled	7.50	16.50
Incense jar	10.00	35.00
Lamp	25.00	62.00
Vase, 12″	12.50	45.00
SCONCES, WALL		
Brass, pair, 2 arms	20.00	45.00
Iron, pair, 2-arm with candleholder	15.00	35.00
SHAVING MUGS		
Farmer plowing	12.00	40.00
Fire engine (steam)	28.50	100.00
Freight car	9.50	45.00
Shoe	9.50	32.50
Tobacco store	22.50	60.00
SILVER, COIN		
Butter knife	4.50	7.50
Dessert spoon	2.50	6.00
Tablespoons, set of 6, marked	20.00	35.00
Teaspoon	2.00	4.00
Tongs, claw ends, 6½″	10.00	17.50

SILVER, VICTORIAN PLATED

Basket, 10¼″ diam., needs resilvering	$5.50	$14.00
Butter dish, good condition	7.50	15.00
Castor set, 5 bottles, unmatched	8.50	15.00
Spoonholder, dinner gong, needs replating	10.00	15.00
Sugar bowl, squat, usable	8.50	11.00
Tea pot, ribbed, needs replating	12.50	16.50
Tea pot, 14″, Reed & Barton, good condition	40.00	67.50

SPATTERWARE

Bowl, pink, peafowl, 3½″ high	30.00	70.00
Cup plate, blue, 4″	8.50	20.00
Cup, child's, green, peafowl	7.00	55.00
Pitcher, 7″, red & blue	45.00	125.00
Plate, 8¼″, "Tulip"	25.00	95.00
Platter, 17¾″ × 14″, blue & red	37.50	100.00
Sugar bowl, covered, tulip	40.00	120.00
Teapot, rainbow	65.00	125.00

STAFFORDSHIRE, HISTORICAL & PICTORIAL

Wm. Adams & Sons:

Cup & saucer, handleless, "Garden Sports"	10.00	24.00
Plate, 7½″, deep pink, "Caledonia"	7.00	15.00

	1950 prices	Present prices
Ralph & James Clews:		
Plate, 7¼", dark blue, "Dr. Syntax Turned Nurse," proof	$21.00	$50.00
Plate, 7-7/8", dark blue, "Landing of Lafayette"	21.00	55.00
Platter, brown, 11" × 13", "Hudson River"	24.00	68.50
J. & J. Jackson:		
Plate, 9", brown, "Water Works Phila"	14.00	42.50
Plate, 10¼", "President's House Wash."	15.00	45.00
Sauce dish, 5", black, "University Hall, Harvard"	15.00	34.00
T. Mayer:		
Bowl, 13", "Arms of Maryland"	190.00	420.00
Plate, 8¾", dark blue, "Arms of Rhode Island"	75.00	160.00
J. & W. Ridgeway:		
Cup & saucer, light blue, Catskill Moss series	12.50	42.50
Plate, 8", dark blue, "Library Phila"	16.00	50.00
Plate, 10", dark blue, "City Hall N.Y."	18.50	59.50

Rogers:		
Plate, 7½", medium blue, "Boston State House"	$16.00	$45.00
Teapot, medium blue, "Boston State House"	40.00	130.00
Joseph Stubbs:		
Plate, 6¾", dark blue, "Woodlands near Phila"	12.00	42.00
Plate, 8¼", dark blue, "Nahant Hotel near Boston"	19.00	48.50
Pitcher, 4½", dark blue, "Boston State House"	35.00	70.00
Platter, 13" × 16", "Mondonhall Ferry"	95.00	160.00
Enoch Wood & Son:		
Cup & saucer, dark blue, impressed, "Wood"	10.00	35.00
Plate, 9¼", dark blue, "B. & O Incline"	37.50	59.50
Plate, 7½", dark blue, "The Capital Washington"	17.50	45.00
Platter, 9¼" × 12", dark blue, "Military Academy, West Point"	135.00	345.00
Platter, 15", dark blue, "Niagara from the American Side"	100.00	225.00

STEINS

Drinking scene, one liter	16.60	35.00

	1950 prices	*Present prices*
Old man bowling, Mettlach, pewter top	$27.00	$45.00
TOLEWARE		
Cake pan, angel	2.50	9.50
Coffee pot, large	4.50	10.00
Lunch basket with tray	2.00	4.50
Matchbox holder, large	1.00	2.75
Scoop	1.00	4.50
Tray, Chippendale border, large	10.00	29.50
TRIVETS		
Arrow, piercing heart	10.00	15.00
Beaded hearts, handled	4.50	7.50
George Washington	10.00	22.50
Good luck	4.50	7.50
Turtle	4.75	9.50
WOODEN WARE		
Bellows, pine	7.00	15.00
Boot jack	2.00	4.00
Butter mold, round, cow	5.50	8.75
Cranberry picker	20.00	40.00
Grain scoop	2.50	8.50
Salt box, hanging, Pennsylvania Dutch	12.50	32.00

4

Market Letter

A theory has been advanced that sales of art and antiques might well be handled by ways similar to sales on the securities markets. We are privileged to be handed a proposed advance sheet of a possible publication having to do with such methods.

THE ARTFUL ANTIQUER

(The real lowdown on the antique and art market)

Publisher's statement: When, as and if this sheet appears on the news stands, *The Wall Street Journal* and the financial section of *The New York Times* are going to be pretty discouraged.

DO YOU COLLECT SEWING TABLE BIRDS?

See us before you make further acquisitions. Our stock is terrific.

Hocus, Pocus and Company
Chippenhook, Vermont and other busy communities. Open around the clock.

YOU HAVE A FRIEND AT BRACE BANTATTAN.

If need be you will be amazed by the things we finance—and at super low interest rates.

BRACE BANTATTAN BANK
New York City and branches at all leading ski areas.

FOR JUST $5.00

We can advise you on how to make a fortune in antiques and art.

LINE OF BULL, INC.

CAREER OPPORTUNITIES

Have you considered a career in chair scraping? Comfortable work right next to a hot stove. Many fringe benefits and old age security.

a profit.

TANGLEWOOD and COMPANY

Buy Majolica, it's going up. Of course we don't mean pieces only ten years old.

TIN, GLAZE and COMPANY

PICASSOS, PICASSOS, PICASSOS.

Our stock is enormous. We are a bit short on his Rose Period but we have a few which, at casual glance, you would think he really painted.

CONFIDENCE ART GALLERY
New York, Ossining, New York
and Leavenworth, Kansas.

DUNCAN PHYFE at his best.

Many items in stock, all attributed to Phyfe. In our opinion as experts we think they should be. So forget Caveat Emptor and consult us first.

YE OLDE FURNITURE SHOPPE

DO YOU NEED A REPRESENTATIVE
IN BUYING OR SELLING ART
AND ANTIQUES?

DOWN BROTHERS HORSEAFLIER AND COMPANY

Offices around the world.
Established *circa* 1690

All our antique wooden tops having been sold to mental institutions, this advertisement is a matter of record only.

TOPPSEY, TURVEY AND COMPANY

5

What Is an Antique?

In any account of the changing prices of antiques over the years, it might be well first to consider what an antique is. There have been import laws regulating customs duties to be paid on antique items coming into this country from abroad and defining antiques for that purpose, but these are actually of concern only to a limited number of dealers and private buyers. Then there is the often heard, "Well, it's a hundred years old, so it's an antique." This, in our opinion, is a poor definition. Mary Greogory glass, delightful but unfortunately much faked, is, if original, of very considerable value and surely antique, although still quite a few years away from being one hundred years old.

Antiques that do qualify for the hundred-year-old definition vary greatly in quality. William Gale and Son, the first silversmiths to use the sterling mark, made, before about 1850, hollow ware not marked sterling; not too long after 1850, they also made hollow ware carrying the sterling mark. All their work was in the best Victorian taste and eminently distinguished. On the other hand, the typical 1840 Empire chest, over one hundred years old to be sure, was in fact one of the worst designed pieces of furniture we have ever gazed upon. Many of the most graceful Victorian pieces of furniture, particularly those copying the French 18th-century motif, are still not quite one hundred years of age.

Items we think of as antiques are items that reveal the personal touch or expression of some individual artist or artisan. The reason they endure well is that they were handmade. Unfortunately, there is very little hand craftsmanship nowadays. The individual touch is lost in factory-made articles, which can never become true antiques.

We frequently hear the remark that antiques are getting scarce. We do not think so, at least as far as fine items are concerned. Witness the stock of the prestigious dealers in cities and in many country areas. And witness the sales in the great auction galleries. Moreover, the dealer exhibits in the better antique shows still fill us with awe and delight. There are, to be sure, certain categories, such as Sèvres soft paste porcelain, that have almost disappeared except in the museums. But there are today an infinite number of fine antiques you can purchase if your pocketbook is up to current market prices.

6

Appraising Antiques

President Meiklejohn of Amherst, in response to student criticism of the way college affairs were conducted, had this to say in chapel one morning more than fifty years ago: "May I say, gentlemen, something about student opinion? Student opinion is always interesting, sometimes valuable, but never decisive."

After many years in appraisal work, we might say that the same holds true of an appraiser's opinion. After his years of examining, handling, and evaluating antiques, the appraisers' opinions on the subject are of more than average authority, but not necessarily decisive. It is a fact that two experienced appraisers can go through a collection, differ on individual items, but come out with approximately the same total.

What the appraiser must avoid is the thought that he is an authority, a real expert about every item coming to his attention. In this respect we have had a most happy experience when we have sought opinions from real authorities. In every instance we experienced the willingness of experts to help us out. In one instance, one of the great authorities on Oriental rugs gave us his opinion on the value of an antique Chinese Oriental of which there was left, following a fire, a piece scarcely over six inches square. We recall items like a pre-Christian-era ceramic camel, a pair of Dorothy Daughty cardinals, and a French silver basket by Odiot; we were helped in our valuations of all these items, without obligations.

Generally speaking, appraisals are made for one of two purposes: estate taxes or insurance. The Internal Revenue Service considers it fair to value items at what might be called a quick-sale price, such as a reliable dealer would pay when buying in quantity—as we express it, "what a willing buyer would give a willing seller."

Appraisals for insurance purposes are made for the purpose of establishing replacement costs in the event of a loss. These are divided into two categories: ordinary insurance and fine-arts coverage. Factory-made items of furniture, for instance, depreciate in the same way as motor cars. The finest modern sofa or motor car becomes "secondhand" and is worth less. A fire insurance adjuster considers original cost and probable life use and settles a claim accordingly, just as a collision-insurance adjuster, in settling for a total wreck, considers the age and market value of that particular automobile.

In appraising for fine-arts coverage, each particular piece is described and valued. Years ago the chief underwriter of a great insurance company told us that his idea of items eligible for fine-arts coverage must have "a continuing value." For instance, a fine Sheraton sofa in original condition and "of the period" (*circa* 1800–1810) might be valued at $800 to $1,000. After five or more years, were it stolen, burned, or irreparably damaged, the replacement cost would be as much or possibly more. Appraisal of fine-arts items accepted by the insurance carrier avoids arguments in case of a loss. In effect, you settle your loss before you have it.

Appraisals do not present too much of a problem if all those involved are "under the sod." We do the best we can giving our honest opinions from the experience we have had. Sometimes our experiences are amusing. Once we started going through the contents of a house with one of the heirs in close attendance. We suppose she had visions of the great wealth in which she would share when the contents were sold. Actually the stuff was not that good. Finally annoyed when she continued to state that our valuations were ridiculously low, we reminded her that although we were not lawyers she was a collateral, not a direct heir, and would be subject to a stiff state inheritance tax. She then changed her tune and expressed her opinion that all our valuations were too high.

One thing that makes things difficult for

an appraiser is the element of sentimental value. Sentimental value has no part of an appraisal, be it antiques or securities. Years ago some of the financially well-fixed old boys along the shores of Long Island Sound would caution their families, "If something happens to me don't ever sell my New Haven stock." As we all know, the stock of the New Haven Railroad has (to put it mildly) not turned out to be a gilt-edged investment. Likewise, many of the antiques held onto for sentimental reasons are not worth what they are thought to be.

At other times we have discovered that folks do not realize how fine some of their things are. We were appraising silver for fine-arts coverage and brought forth a tall two-handled cup. We were impressed and remarked that it should be good. The lady owner informed us that it was an odd item from her late mother and of no consequence. We followed a narrow rim around the base and came to the very clear mark D.V.V. (Daniel van Voorhis, one of the great Philadelphia silversmiths). The good lady was aghast when she saw our valuation.

7

Fakes & Phonies— Honest & Otherwise

We know of a dealer who sells furniture at reputable antique shows completely "made up." The dealer's husband is not only a competent cabinetmaker but also has a sense of fine taste and design. We remember a small and most attractive four-drawer chest with a fine straight-bracket base. This had been fashioned from a commode (not lift top) which in itself had little value except for storage. Other items in this dealer's many exhibits have included schoolmaster's desks, stands, benches, farrier's boxes, and pipe and spoon racks. All these things are sold honestly for what they are, without mis-presentation and at modest prices. While they might not satisfy those with a craving for "genuine antiques," they make interesting and attractive additions to any home.

Years ago we visited with a New York dealer who handles both authentic antique furniture and fine copies made up in his own shop. The wood has been "aged" by being sunk in the New Jersey salt marshes. The workmanship is superb, and it takes an expert to spot the difference. The average person has some difficulty in determining what is an original and what is a good copy. (One test for the novice, in the case of round-top tables, is to measure the diameter in all directions. If it is the same, the chances are it is a made-up piece. Wood shrinks contrary to the grain, and a really old top will measure one half to a full inch less across the grain.) Our dealer friend was perfectly honest, but he was doing a sizable wholesale business and voiced the opinion that certain fine copies going to dealers ended up in their shops labeled as completely original and of the period.

We are not dealers, but we do sell on commission for others in estate sales and individual items handed us for disposal. Recently we sold to a dealer a satin glass pitcher and four tumblers, shaded deep pink to off-white, all in proof condition. We were startled to hear from the purchasing dealer that they had been judged reproductions. We are not qualified as experts on satin glass, but the items came from an old and respected family. They were wedding gifts to the lady's grandmother, who would be over one hundred if living and was married at the early age of eighteen. At one hundred, the late lamented grandma would have been born in 1868 and married in 1886. Some expert says the pitcher is too heavy and the pontil not right. Maybe so, but we doubt that they were reproduced in 1886, the year satin glass was brought to perfection by an Englishman named Webb.

We contend that most successful dealers are honest because they know that it pays off in the long run, regardless of any other consideration. But honest dealers do make honest mistakes, fooled like all the rest of us sometimes. And of course there are exceptions to the rule. One thing that might arouse our suspicion is the matter of quantity. If we notice a dealer's booth just crammed with cranberry glass and Mary Gregory, we do wonder where it all came from.

There is, apparently, an influx of reproductions in glass from Europe, and very well done they are, ranging from elaborate pairs of lustres to goblets and wines. One has to be careful. One story, perhaps apocryphal, we have heard is about a dealer who exhibited a dozen Morning Glory wine goblets in his shop at $10 each. A customer said he would take them if the dealer would furnish a written guarantee that they were "of the period." "Well, I kind of like those wines and guess I will keep them," was the dealer's reply. (The wines might have sold better put out one at a time and higher priced. We once sold, to a dealer, a footed Morning Glory tall tumbler, with a small nick in the base, for $40.)

Another story that we know to be true

concerns some canary "Sandwich glass" items totaling about $100 wholesale. The purchasing dealer, about to make out her check to the dealer across the aisle, took another knowledgeable look, and back they went—all reproductions.

Years ago we went to see a very distinguished worker in gold leaf. His shop was in a ramshackle building on the east side of New York. As we came to the top of the stairs and started to turn toward the gilder's workshop, we saw, straight ahead, a sign on a door of another shop: "We put marks and monograms on porcelain and pottery." And so they do. They also take marks such as "Made in China" *off* the bases of Rose Medallion and Rose Canton.

That day the gilder had just finished a Louis XV console for the entrance hall of a fashionable New York apartment. Particles of gold leaf had "worn off," showing the red burnishing clay. You would swear it was a real antique. The distinguished dealer was an honest gentleman, but we wonder if the apartment owners might just say, "How do you like our console? We picked it up in a little shop near the Tuileries."

At a famous exhibit of Sèvres porcelain outside Paris, the son of Sampson, standing on the sidelines, remarked, "People don't know it, but my father made some of those pieces." Sampson of Paris was an all-time-great reproducer of Sèvres porcelain. Mostly he marked his stuff, and the Sampson mark is sufficient in itself to bring a high price.

In the case of furniture, we more or less divide items into three categories: originals (of the period), acknowledged reproductions, and fine copies. We have two chairs, a ribbon-back Chippendale and a Hepplewhite shield back that we class as fine copies. The wood is dense Santo Domingo mahogany; the carving, molding, and so forth is excellent. The seat rails are stamped T. Robinson and Sons. Father purchased them from Robinson (Cambridge, Mass.) in 1910, paying $18 each, with muslin covers on the seats. To the casual observer, by appearance and weight they look "of the period." In any case, they are worth more than $18 each.

Proving the authenticity of antiques is sometimes fun. We were managing an antique exhibit for the Rutland, Vermont, State Fair. Exhibits by private owners were judged on individual merit, and cash premiums were awarded. A youngster brought in some plates, obviously not too old or too good. We inquired, "Who owns the plates?" "My mother. They are old. She has had them all her life." "And how old is your mother?" "She's eighty-five." "And how old are you?" "Fifteen." We made what seemed to be the appropriate comment: "Well, young man, you have a remarkable mother!"

Bernard Berenson graduated from Harvard in 1887. He went on to become one of the world's greatest authorities on the paintings of the old masters. His book *Italian Painters of the Renaissance* was the last word in reference books. He was the adviser to the greatest (and richest) collectors. He was the friend and guide of Isabella Stewart Gardner in her collection of art for Fenway Court, in Boston. To Lord Duveen he acted for thirty years as the one person who authenticated paintings that

Lord Duveen was selling to his customers. Duveen was probably the world's greatest salesman of fine paintings. His customers were individuals of enormous wealth. The price was no object, but they wanted to be sure they were not getting "stuck." This association with Duveen was mutually helpful to both and especially helpful to Berenson financially. The combination finally broke up when Duveen was trying to sell a painting to Andrew Mellon as a Giorgione. Berenson refused to certify it as such and insisted that it was a Titian. Mellon had enough Titians and wanted a Giorgione. (Titian and Giorgione were both tremendous painters, but Titian lived to be over ninety, worked hard, and had a tremendous output. Giorgione died young, and the scarcity of his works makes them far more valuable.) Berenson's refusal to certify made Duveen furious, and a friendship of thirty years ended then and there.

The breakup of Lord Duveen and Bernard Berenson is a classic example of the bitter feelings that can be engendered by a difference of opinion in judging paintings. Perhaps one reason is the amount of money involved. Off-hand we can think of no piece of furniture that has sold for more money than the Van Pelt highboy sold in the Reifsnyder sale for $44,000. In the field of paintings forty-odd thousand dollars is just "peanuts." Great canvases have now gone into the millions.

With so much money involved, the temptation to market fakes has of course greatly increased. There are several suits now in the courts involving hundreds of thousands of dollars. And some of the fakers, like the central European caught faking Vermeer, are very good. Some of the experts examined this man's Vermeer and said the examples were too good, no living person could possibly do such a great job. The accused, his ability questioned, said, "Furnish me the materials and I will show you." So, in jail, he was supplied canvas, paints, and brushes and proved to the experts that he could repeat his performance of a marvelous fake.

In no field of antiques is there such a difference of opinion among experts. A Goddard or a Townsend or a Savery will, even if unlabeled, get the consensus of opinion of experts that such and such a piece of furniture was undoubtedly made by this or that designer and craftsman. But with art, the varied opinions by the experts are, to say the least, confusing.

Quite recently the career of the most successful art forger of all times has come to light. From about 1946 to 1961 this painter faked over one thousand drawings and paintings under so many pseudonyms that the few art dealers who detected single forgeries failed to link them with the painter. Most of the fakes were the alleged work of the French Impressionists. From about 1961 on, the forger started to get into trouble because of his connections with two art dealers even more crooked than he. One of the interesting aspects of the painter's work was the fact that, although an artist of real ability, he was unable to market his own original works. No one was interested. But his fakes of great and well-known artists sold like hotcakes.

Drawings and oils were sold to an art museum and to some prestigious art dealers in New York, Chicago, and elsewhere; a large "collection" went to a southern millionaire who purchased in good faith to present these works to a university. In the meantime the two crooked art dealers who were peddling the work of the artist on a commission basis were going a good job of gypping him. Once the faker became suspicious that he was not getting his proper percentage. To check, he called a great art gallery that had advertised a Matisse oil, saying that he was a collector and interested in purchasing the painting. He was informed that it had been sold. Inquiring the price, he was aghast to be told that it was about $60,000. He asked if that were not a little high and got this reply: "A Matisse of that quality, you know, is rarely placed on the market."

Eventually, of course, the fakes and the faker were discovered; the forger landed in a Spanish jail, but was released two months later pending further evidence. The fine old art galleries which had unknowingly sold the fake items in every case refunded the purchase price to the buyer, as they always do if a mistake has been made. The larger concerns could take this in their stride, but some smaller dealers were really hurt.

8

Auctions

Everyone has heard auction stories, like the one about the man at a country auction who raised his hand to scratch his nose and found himself the successful bidder for a chamber pot knocked down to him for fifty cents.

Country auctions are fun, a good show. Dealers like them because things of the pots-and-pans variety go for ridiculous prices, considering their actual worth, while items of real value are sometimes missed by the majority of the particular crowd attending. We know of a dealer who bid successfully for a curly maple candle-stand, in fine condition, with a gracefully turned pedestal column and excellent snake feet; it was knocked down to him for $75. We have seen candlestands not as good, in our opinions, priced for sale at $250.

Some years back we attended a country auction at which George Durrie's painting *Home for Thanksgiving* was put up. The auctioneer, not too much up on art, inquired if anyone would start the bidding at $100. It was started all right, and the painting went for $2,600. (Currier and Ives large folio prints from this painting now go for more than the $2,600 paid for the painting.) The auctioneer was almost overcome and had to be assisted to an adjoining woodshed and given a drink of cold water.

Bargains can also be obtained in the great city galleries by dealers who have patience and know-how. We know a dealer in early silver who will sit for hours in a great auction gallery without making a move. Then a tea set or some important item of hollow ware will come up, the bidding will lag, and our dealer friend will get a bargain.

There is an excitement, a certain tension,

during the bidding for important items. The dealers, private buyers, or their agents, not wishing to divulge their identity to competitive bidders, have prearranged signals to the presiding auctioneer in a big sale of really important items. It might be a shifting of spectacles, a movement of hand to face, or other gestures.

Mr. Rorimer, representing the Metropolitan Museum of Art, was the successful bidder for the great Rembrandt canvas *Aristotle Contemplating the Bust of Homer* at well over $2 million. He said afterwards, "I knew I had gone beyond the limit of what we had to spend. But our credit is good. And we have friends who will help out to make up what we are short."

Purchases at auctions, or elsewhere, are subject pricewise to what the purchaser most desires. At the same auction where Mr. Rorimer made his successful bid, a garden scene by Renoir went for $200,000. If we had "all the money in the world," our choice for our own pleasure would be the Renoir over the Rembrandt canvas, despite the fact that the latter sold for more than ten times as much.

Auction bids for great paintings have gone to astronomical heights. In many cases there is no record of what the artist was paid for his work. In some cases we do know. Monet was paid $80 for *La Terrace à St. Addresse,* sold not too long ago in London (also to a representative of the Metropolitan) for $1,400,000. This price for a French Impressionist has since been topped by about $150,000 for Renoir's *Pont des Artes.* We do not know what Renoir was originally paid for the painting. But we do know that Renoir painted it at the fairly early age of thirty-four and that it was not necessarily as good as some of his later work.

We had about two hours to spend between lunch and a late Saturday afternoon June wedding. We stopped in at an important sale at a great auction gallery. We were intrigued by the result of the bidding for a pair of 18th-century cut-crystal chandeliers. A lady standing in the back of the room, with sables to the floor, a hat about a yard in diameter, and a cigarette holder almost that long, entered the bidding. The auction was for one piece, the successful bidder to take two at the same price if he or she desired. As the bidding progressed the lady stayed in, and when she raised her cigarette holder for the last time to become the successful bidder at $4,100, the auctioneer thanked her and inquired, "One or two?" The lady raised her hand in a combination victory sign and her desire to purchase both chandeliers.

At the same sale a Tompkins tall clock went for $4,500. That fall we were in New York and remarked to a dealer friend whose firm handles English items that it was a good price for the clock. He informed us that his firm had dropped out of the bidding at $4,000 and probably should have stayed in. It seems they had had a cable from a London dealer who assumed they had bought the clock to inquire if they wished to take a 20 percent profit on their purchase. The firm telephoned the actual purchaser, a private individual, to inquire if he would care to take a profit. His answer was in the negative, since he bought the clock for his own pleasure.

In the valuation for estate-tax purposes of items to be sold at auction, the appraiser estimates what should be considered a fair price plus about 20 percent, which would be the cost to the estate of selling the items. We once made a goof when we valued things to be sold by a fine auctioneer with a great following. It was good stuff but either better than we thought or picked up by an enthusiastic attendance whose checking accounts seemed to be unlimited. Our appraisal was about $45,000, including the cost of selling. The total figure for all things sold was $55,000.

One of the amusing scenes we have witnessed at auctions was at a sale in a country town with a wealth of fine items. A distant relative, a lady a little on the roly-poly side in figure, wanted sixteen cranberry wines etched with the family crest. When they came up, the lady arose from her seat and started the bidding with a kind of no-nonsense attitude. But there were several others who also craved cranberry wines. The competition was fast and furious, and the price went up rapidly. But the little lady held her ground, and when she finally became the successful bidder the whole crowd arose to give her a standing ovation.

9

For Fun, Money, or Marbles

Our appraisal work has always been well remunerated, together with side benefits of delicious meals and enjoyable conversation. We also remember some amusing incidents. We went to do an insurance appraisal of items in a country home—really fabulous early antiques. Remembering our smoking habits, we did not look forward to going the whole day without a smoke because the charming lady was a minister's wife and no doubt disapproved of smoking. We had hardly started our job when she lit up a cigarette. And as the luncheon hour approached she remarked, "Well, it is about time for some sherry." The only way we could explain it was that the minister was a Unitarian. (Unitarians, according to some folks brought up in that church, are supposed to have one foot in hell and the other on a banana peel.) Another older lady for whom we did an appraisal remarked, "It is almost time for lunch. I rarely drink in the middle of the day, but don't you think we had better have one?" It was a good stiff one.

Appraisal work is something more than just earning a living. It is like watching a parade of beautiful, interesting objects. It is "better than a play." In examining figures in this passing parade, one attempts to fix values fair to both the government and the estate in tax appraisals, replacement prices in insurance appraisals, and an estimate of what they might sell for when we are consulted about the possibility of a sale.

Too many instances come up to even touch on their highlights. But occasionally one of perhaps unusual interest comes up. About fifteen years ago we appraised the contents of a New York apartment and a country place, both owned by a charming couple. Since then all these items have been transferred to a single residence. Our first appraisal was for insurance purposes, and recently we have reappraised them for the same purpose. It is interesting to note that the owners spent some years in France, had an interest in 18th- and early 19th-century French antiques, and so the collection has an unusual preponderance of French items. French items of the 18th century are much sought after and have risen tremendously in value. We list below a very limited number of items from our first appraisal and our recent reappraisal:

	15 years ago	*Today*
French oak dresser, 18th century	$450.00	$1,200.00
French cabinet, "Bonnetiere," 18th century	250.00	600.00
French corner chair, 18th century	150.00	350.00
French armchairs, pair, 18th century	600.00	1,000.00
Pine tavern table, American	150.00	250.00

	15 years ago	*Today*
French wooden wall salt container	$25.00	$45.00
French wooden wall flour container	25.00	45.00
French 3-branch pewter lamp	200.00	300.00
Hanging shelves, French, 18th century	50.00	150.00
Pair French lamps from pewter candlesticks	40.00	90.00
Pair French pewter chocolate pots	50.00	100.00
French pewter soup tureen	50.00	125.00
French pewter lavabo	300.00	425.00
Oil on canvas, Breton woman	150.00	250.00
Painting of boys in Napoleonic costumes	100.00	150.00
Oil on canvas, by Diaz	150.00	450.00
Guy Arnoux posters (3)	75.00	120.00
Regency card table, English	450.00	1,000.00

Not all are dyed-in-the-wool antique fans. In 1948 we had a delightful visit on a railway car out of Boston with our old professor, Robert Frost. A course with Mr. Frost was easily worth an entire year's college tuition. After inquiring politely about our activities with antiques, he made this comment, "Well, I have an old Morris chair that I think a good deal of."

Mr. Frost wrote:

> And I shall return
> If dissatisfied
> With what I learn
> From having died.

He has not returned. Perhaps he found an old Morris chair.

10

Buying & Selling Antiques

Years ago we knew a dealer, a lady of unquestioned honesty and real knowledge of what was good (or was not), who had an unusual method of handling individual items offered her to purchase. She would examine the article and then state to the prospective seller, "I believe I can get so much for this in my shop. I can offer you so much (naming a figure to gross her a 25 to 30 percent profit.)" We believe that in the long run she generated a greater profit than the cadgy dealer always looking to buy something to "double his money."

On the other hand, a dealer attempting to

buy things from a private seller is confronted with the fact that most private sellers disregard the dealer's problems: that he has a business and must consider interest on his money, risk of damage, and routine expenses such as rent on the shop and various other costs of maintaining and running a business. Many private sellers do not take this into consideration. They expect dealers to pay them top retail price, forgetting the dealer's right to make a fair profit for his expense and risk.

Dealers do a large volume of business with other dealers. They mark up their wares so that they can offer another dealer a discount and be in a position to dicker with private buyers on the price. Perhaps this is the only way the antique business can be conducted.

In selling antiques and art in quantity there is something to be said in favor of an auction and other things in favor of a so-called estate sale, where all items are price-marked. We are not auctioneers, but we have had a considerable experience with estate sales, where we sell on commission. We do believe that many private buyers give too much attention to the price mark and too little to the quality of the item being offered. One can throw away $25 on one item and get a real bargain on another priced at $100. In this respect we think the dealers are smarter. They consider the price tag, of course, but they compare it with the quality and desirability of the item and what it might bring if purchased and held for the right buyer or collector. Just recently we had left over from an estate sale a cut-glass covered butter dish in proof condition and of really fabulous deep brilliant cut. It was priced at $45, and no one paid attention to it. We carried it along and sold it to a dealer. She never quibbled about the price of $45 and sold it the same afternoon to a collector for $80.

The average private buyer of antiques or art is not investing his or her money in a crap game. Rightfully, folks wish to know about the quality, authenticity, or whatever one likes to call it, of what they are purchasing. The reliability of the selling dealer is most important. No doubt there are places in New York where one might purchase a fine diamond or an emerald for a price somewhat less than that charged by one of the fine old prestigious shops. The same holds true of early silver, 18th-century furniture, or Victorian art glass. But the average purchaser is not a gem expert or an authority on silver, glass, or furniture. Fine art and good antiques cost real money, and one should not shop around for a little lower price in exchange for doing business with a dealer of established reputation and in whom one may have confidence. Even the finest of dealers can on rare occasions make a mistake, but they are the quickest in their willingness to rectify an error.

Having been satisfied on the quality of an item whose purchase is being considered and the price having been reconciled with the size of one's checking account, there is still the most important consideration: Do you really like it? And will it go well where you intend to use it in your home? Of course there are some occasions, cases of "love at first sight," when one disregards the checking account balance and says, "This I must have!" It becomes a cherished possession and never causes regret.

11

"*Antiquers*"

A lady of fairly recently acquired wealth was asked if she and her husband had any antiques. "Oh no, Frank will not let me buy anything secondhand," she answered.

We know of a family of culture and intelligence whose home is in good taste and altogether charming. But there is scarcely an antique in the place. Being of Yankee origin, our minds run to what these finely made and obviously expensive items would bring at sale, compared with what they cost. The answer is a comparatively small percentage. We have discovered this over the years when we have had, in our estate sales, the finest (but modern) furniture.

"Antiquers"

We guess that to be an "antiquer" you must have had it in your blood for some time. The great depression raised havoc with our family's finances but fortunately did not take away the antiques. Over the years we have enjoyed them, and our children are enjoying our surplus of such things. And their monetary value, of course, has increased immeasurably.

In the evening as we sit reading, we can look across the room at a most graceful Queen Anne side chair, all original. And farther away in the dining room we can see a swell-front Hepplewhite cherry chest, in our family since 1790. To its right is a Sheraton secretary desk whose cubbyholes served as mail boxes for a small Vermont town of about nine families. To its left, on a Hepplewhite card table, is a Staffordshire tureen transfer-decorated in pale blue with English scenes. And over a cabinet in the living room is a Staffordshire poodle that was of great sentimental value to Grandma because, as she informed us, she used to look up at it when Grandpa was "courting" her on the family couch.

We do have a few reproductions: a

shield-back Hepplewhite armchair and an armchair of French make with graceful curving arms of mahogany with a center inlay of satinwood. These chairs were in the main drawing room of a fine old country place. We had always admired them, and one evening after we had been entertained at dinner we expressed the thought that we wished we owned them. Our older and very good friend, a lady of real charm, said, "All the things in the house are in a trust and I cannot give them away. But I do have the privilege of selling them." We inquired cautiously, "How much for the two chairs?" "Oh," said she, "two dollars and a half."

Among antiquers there are always a certain number of collectors. Their hobby for collecting runs to almost every conceivable item of interest or merit—and sometimes a little less on the merit side. A great many dealers have customers who are collectors. So they are always on the lookout for things with appeal to their collector customers. Years ago we had a dealer friend with a customer who collected left-handed mustache cups. Amazingly enough, she located a good number over a period of time.

A friend of ours, a gentleman of some wealth, was a collector of silver with a special liking for the work of Henry Chawner. Price was no consideration when a Chawner piece came on the market. Very recently we saw another dealer pay a rather fancy price for a piece of Hawkes-marked cut glass. He told us that his collector customer would give him a fair profit on any piece so marked, even if it had a slight imperfection.

We are not collectors but have thought that it would be fun to collect drinking receptacles. An old-fashioned glass once used by Franklin D. Roosevelt or a highball glass of Sir Winston Churchill's would be interesting and probably worth money. And then there was Anna Held's slipper, from which her wealthy gentleman boy friend drank champagne. We wonder what became of the slipper. We do know of a blown high wine with twist stem that was supposed to have been used by George Washington. But could you prove it?

Youthful collectors—young married folks—soon discover that furnishing a small home or an apartment with good modern furniture is expensive and (looking to the future) that the depreciation in values is quite rapid. These young people of taste and discrimination, with a good financial future but without immediate funds to patronize the great auction galleries, find other ways to acquire what they need. In New York away east or down in the Village there are auction galleries and sales rooms where pieces of some age, substance, and charm can be purchased at prices within limited incomes. and all over the country dealers have barns and sheds filled with furniture "in the rough," needing a good deal of attention but fundamentally of good design. There is a lively interest in taking these things home to "do over" and restore, with end-result items both useful and of real charm and with enhanced and continuing value. Years ago we were concerned with ventilation in removing old paint: finish and slow-drying varnish looked fine when applied but collected every dust particle in the air. Materials are now available which eliminate the necessity of ventilation and dust-proof rooms. An apartment kitchen has become a most satisfactory workshop.

12

Hi-ho Silver

Rather frequently, when we have been about to conduct an estate sale, we have mentioned silver items coming up. Usually we seem to hear this comment: "Silver. That's the last thing I want. Too much work to take care of it." And yet when the sale comes up, silver sells like popcorn at the movies. Odd sterling serving pieces and hollow ware go fast. Flatware is not so good a seller unless certain patterns are spotted by folks who are short in the same pattern or are trying to expand the numbers of what they have at hand.

Early silver—by distinguished silversmiths, American, English, or French,—comes up in sales at the great auction galleries or is found in certain prestigious city shops. It is rarely seen in antique shows or at the shops of smaller dealers around the country. As one dealer remarked to us, "If we get a piece of good early silver we can sell it over the telephone." Another reason why less silver is offered for sale has to do with the liquidation of estates. Heirs do not know what to do with such things as sofas and other large furniture pieces. But they can always make room for more silver, and quite often family sentiment is involved. Around 1790, for example, a girl named Patience Walker married Lemuel Farwell. We have some of their flat silver: good coin silver but not by any famous maker and of no great intrinsic value. But they are of sentimental value and also a little amusing. The pieces are not monogrammed, but each one is engraved "P. W. Farwell." Patience apparently was taking no chances on not being able to identify her stuff.

The work of the early American silversmiths had a great simplicity of design.

Later on, when the Victorians wanted something more fancy, they adorned the plain surfaces of teapots, cans, and flagons with heavy and intricate engraving. The work was beautifully done, but of course it spoiled the value of the pieces in the eyes of collectors.

From our own experience in estate sales (in this case, going back only a few years), we can list what ordinary sterling items were bringing and what they go for now:

	Five years ago	*Today*
Bonbon dishes	$10.00	$15.00
Bread trays (some small dents)	5.00	15.00
Sterling bowls (heavy and ornate)	30.00	45.00
Pitchers (9), 1½ pts.	60.00	95.00
Revere reproduction bowls	45.00	60.00
Bread-and-butter plates (in sets, each)	3.50	7.50
Pair serving pieces	26.00	30.00

(*Note*: In hollow ware, if it is heavy and not dented or pitted, it seems to make little difference if the piece has been monogrammed.)

In the sale of fine, early American silver, the name of the maker has a great deal to do with the price buyers are willing to pay. Recently in a great city auction gallery a teapot by Samuel Casey went for $12,000. It was of very fine quality, but Casey does not, of course, have the name of Paul Revere. In the same sale sugar tongs by Paul Revere went for $5,259, estimated at probably five times the price if the mark had been that of another maker. The price of a teapot similar to Casey's by Paul Revere would have been astronomical, depending perhaps on the size of some buyer's checking account.

In our own experience we know of a pair of about seven-inch footed salvers with a Chippendale edge purchased years ago for $500, appraised eleven years ago at $800, and we would suppose valued today at $1,500. And we know of a matching pair of porringers (unusually deep) by John Vernon (New York, 1970), sold for $1,000 twelve years ago and now conservatively worth $2,500. Current offerings of antique silver by such makers as Robert Hennel, Eben Coker, the Batemans, and others are priced, conservatively, at a 30 percent increase over prices paid just five years ago.

We have in our files price catalogues of a collection of English silver, mostly by Hester Bateman and other members of the Bateman family, sold in 1958, and a collection of American silver, predominantly Philadelphia-made, sold in 1955. We list below the actual sale prices received and, opposite, a conservative estimate of what the pieces from the two sales might bring today:

1955 SALE, AMERICAN SILVER

	1955 prices	*Today's prices*
Pear-shaped coffee pot, Joubert (Paris, 1784)	$250.00	$600.00
Dessert spoon, Myer Myers (New York, 1793–95)	40.00	75.00
Wine funnel, Robert Swan (Massachusetts, 1795)	25.00	35.00
Pear-shaped can, Jos. Foster (Boston, 1760–1839)	140.00	260.00
Repousse tea service, 4-piece, New York, 1850	150.00	250.00
Sugar nippers, 4 pairs, Philip Syng, Jr. (Philadelphia, 1770–90)	250.00	400.00

	1955 prices	*Today's prices*
Tablespoons, 12, Jos. Richardson & others (Philadelphia, 1790)	$45.00	$120.00
Buckles & combs, 5, Richardson & others	65.00	175.00
Tea caddy, Jos. Lownes (Philadelphia, 1790)	225.00	350.00
Pear-shaped can, Philip Syng, Sr. (Philadelphia, 1676–1739)	1,000.00	2,000.00
Pear-shaped creamer, Daniel van Voorhis (Philadelphia, 1782)	375.00	550.00
Pear-shaped can, Samuel Soumain (Philadelphia, 1754–65)	300.00	450.00
Sugar urn, Jos. Lownes	350.00	500.00
Porringer, Jos. Richardson, Sr. (Philadelphia, 1711–84)	525.00	1,000.00
Sauce boats, pair, Philip Syng, Jr.	2,100.00	3,500.00
Flat top tankard, Wm. Vilant (Philadelphia, 1725)	3,500.00	4,500.00
Pyriform coffee pot, Philip Syng, Jr.	4,000.00	7.500.00

1958 SALE, ENGLISH SILVER

Serving implements, 6, Hester Bateman (London, 1774–93)	$170.00	$210.0
Ajoure cake servers, 2; serving spoons, 6, Hester Bateman	150.00	260.00
Mugs, 4, Peter, Ann & William Bateman (London, 1791–1801)	200.00	300.00
Fox head stirrup cup & ale mug, Hester Bateman, 1782 & 1794	270.00	375.00
Chamber candlestick, Hester Bateman, 1790	130.00	225.00
Dish cross, Hester Bateman, 1788	230.00	350.00
Wine funnels, 4, Hester Bateman, 1777–82	100.00	140.00
Ajoure cruet, 8 silver mounted bottles, Hester Bateman, 1780	230.00	450.00
Chamber candlesticks, 2, Hester Bateman, 1780 & 1782	170.00	350.00
Ajoure sweetmeat baskets, 2, Hester Bateman, 1788 & 1789	160.00	225.00
Engraved argyle, Hester Bateman, 1778	210.00	325.00

	1958 prices	*Today's prices*
Standish, Hester Bateman, 1787	$200.00	$300.00
Engraved ewer-form hot water jug, Peter & Ann Bateman, 1794	150.00	200.00
Ajoure sweetmeat urns, 2, Hester Bateman, 1780–81	225.00	350.00
Ajoure cruet, Wm. Sutton (London, 1793)	90.00	150.00
Engraved tea service, 4-piece, Hester Bateman, 1781–91	525.00	850.00
Circular tray, 16-inch, footed, Peter & Ann Bateman, 1796	400.00	800.00

It might be helpful to note the difference in the marking of American and British silver. Usually the best we can do with American silversmiths is to establish a working period. This comes from their advertisements, from the places where they were located and the time when they worked, and from various town and city records and other historical information. It is practically impossible to give the exact year that an item was made by an American silversmith.

The British had a far better method of marking. Each piece made had to be registered with an assay office, as for instance the leopard's head for the London office, the anchor for Birmingham, or the harp for Dublin. The *lion-passant* mark showed that the piece was "real silver" (the same content as our sterling). The date letter can be easily looked up and shows the exact year the piece was made. English silver was taxed from 1784 to 1890. For the first two years of this period, it bore the king's head and then the queen's head. In addition, the maker's mark can, in a surprising number of cases, be identified.

The marks on French and other continental silver are a little more complicated to identify and not of as much general interest as American and English silver.

13

We Like 'Em Voluptuous

We were about to do an appraisal of the contents of a country place for fine-arts insurance coverage. At a casual glance we could see interesting early items of furniture, brass, iron, copper, and wooden ware appropriate for a home in the country. We felt we had some knowledge of the value of those items. But we were not so sure about the art items hanging on the walls. We suggested that the lady of the house give us a quick tour and rundown of the paintings.

We started in and shortly came to what seemed a bit unintelligible to us. "This," we were pridefully informed, "is our nude."

With our perhaps unfortunate lack of proper appreciation we commented, "She does not look very voluptuous."

We are, no doubt, almost completely lacking in expertise as far as art is concerned. But we do have our likes and dislikes. We are unable to go into raptures over Marcel DuChamp's *Nude Descending a Staircase*. And whether they are hanging on the wall in a painting or walking around in the flesh, we like to see girls looking like females and men looking like males. Certainly this has little to do with sex appeal. One of the most delightful paintings we know of is an oil on canvas of a little old Breton peasant lady wearing a white cap, surely not exactly "sexy."

The art market, at the moment, might well be described as "wild and woolly." The participants include prominent collectors, museums, distinguished dealers, and art experts, along with dealers not so distinguished, fake artists, those interested in art purely for speculative purposes, and a certain number of the "look-along" general public. An amusing story is told of a Paris dealer who had a telephone order from a customer for two Matisses. Asked if he would like to look at the paintings, the customer's reply was, "When I buy one hundred shares of Royal Dutch I don't go out and look at the oil wells."

Perhaps the start of the recent rise in art prices was the sale at Parke-Bernet of art in the estate of the widow of Alfred William Erickson in November 1961. It was a short sale lasting barely sixty minutes, but the treasures sold were of the utmost importance.

Rembrandt's *Aristotle Contemplating the Bust of Homer* had been purchased in 1928 by the Ericksons from Lord Duveen for \$750,000, sold back to Duveen in 1929 for \$500,000, and purchased again in 1936 for \$590,000. At the 1961 sale, bidding started at \$1 million. Mr. James Rorimer, who represented the Metropolitan Museum of Art, was the successful purchaser at \$2,300,000. Crivelli's *Madonna and Child* (1474) brought \$220,000. In 1886 the painting was sold at Christie's in London for the equivalent of about \$650 in our money at the then going rate of exchange.

Hals's *Man with a Herring* brought

$145,000, more than three times as much as the Ericksons paid for it in 1925. Fragonard's *Girl Reading* fetched $875,000, twice what any Fragonard had ever brought. This delicate painting has a breath-taking beauty. It was reported that when it appeared on the velvet block the audience suddenly burst into applause.

Fine art can go down as well as up. Nattier's *La Marquise de Baglion as Flora* went for $175,000 after a long decline in Nattier's work from the $240,000 price paid for it in 1927. A Gainsborough that cost $300,000 in 1928 went for $35,000, and a Van Dyck purchased for $200,000, plus two paintings thrown in, went for $27,000.

Prices in the art market are governed by two elements: the state of the economy, and tastes, both subject to change. The Erickson sale demonstrated that the economy was good, or even better, but that in some instances tastes had changed.

Aristotle, commissioned in 1653 by a Sicilian noble for 400 florins (estimated $7,800) and sold in 1961 for $2,300,000, might be considered a good investment.

But this would depend on how much you like the painting. But from another standpoint, $7,800 invested in the middle of the 17th century at 4 percent interest compounded annually would be $1,020,000,000 in 1961.

We know something about the economy. We know that things were good in 1961, and for the most part things have boomed since then. But there's an old saying that there is no accounting for taste. It was taste that caused one man to pay 800,000 gold frances (about $1 million in purchasing power today) for a Millet that might bring $20,000 today. A London art gallery paid a huge price for Edwin Landseer's *Monarch of the Glen*. And you do not have to be extremely old to remember when Rosa Bonheur's horses were "the thing" (we have heard rumors that they are coming back).

In the past ten years, French Impressionists have been the "big deal." There might be several reasons for it. One, certainly, is the continuing booming economy. Or possibly the acquisition of outstanding "old masters" by museums and their consequent permanent withdrawal from the art market has made a certain kind of art scarce. And it might just be that those with really important money to spend are, like us, more attracted by colorful country, garden, and village scenes with interesting characters than by depicted flocks of angels.

In 1959 Renoir's *The Daughters of Durand-Ruel* brought $225,000. Thirty-four years earlier a major Renoir could be had for less than $2,000, and in 1942 the top price was $24,000. In the sale of the Goldschmidt collection in 1958, Manet's *Rue de Berne* went for $316,400. One like it sold for $30 in 1884, and in the early 1950's an average Manet fetched $24,000. From the same collection Cézanne's *Boy in a Red Vest* was sold for $616,000. A Paris dealer received $600 for the same painting in 1900. Van Gogh's *Public Garden at Arles* was sold in 1958 for $369,600, or $363,600 more than a Van Gogh brought in 1927. In his entire lifetime Van Gogh sold only two paintings.

14

"Put In Some Cold Water"

Father was a person of intelligence with some knowledge of and great respect for mathematics and Latin. He was a fine penman, had a good knowledge of the securities markets, and could analyze the most complicated balance sheet. His avocations were fly fishing, gardening, and finishing work on fine furniture, all of which he did well. But he never could, or would, make out what went on in an internal combustion engine. We had some interesting cars, and father's only remedy if the engine did not perform properly was to pour some cold water into the radiator.

Our first automobile was a 1913 Model T. Father learned to drive on a 1914 Jeffrey. He decided that one might as well start doing everything at once. So before he really caught on to steering the car, he was busily engaged in shifting gears and trampling on the accelerator (usually too hard). His idea of steering was: if the car was going in one direction, "reefer" with the steering wheel to go in the other direction. His children remember riding up School Street with father at the wheel, the car careening in a zigzag course and ladies standing on the front stoops of their houses and screaming to their children to get out of the way. Father loved to drive and was probably one of the world's worst drivers. To quote Ralph Nader, riding with father was "unsafe at any speed." But amazingly, he never had any accidents, no collisions, or even a scraped fender. Perhaps other drivers saw him coming and took refuge in the nearest ditch.

There is today a tremendous interest in antique and classic cars. We wonder what the cars in our family would bring today if we had kept them. We had several Ford

Model T coupés, a Dodge three-passenger coupé, an open Cadillac phaeton, and a 1922 Cadillac brougham with custom body. But the prize package was a 1920 Pierce-Arrow touring car with jump seats. It had the large 48-horsepower engine (big bore, short stroke), an all-aluminum body, crank case, and transmission housing. One like it sold in 1967 for $11,000.

Fantastic prices have been and are being paid for antique and classic cars. A 1913 Henderson Opera Coupé originally sold new for $2,285 brought $8,500 at a 1966 auction. Probably the world record auction price for an old car was $31,000 for a Stanley Steamer Mountain Wagon (open body with seats crosswise, four in all).

Here are some 1967 auction prices paid for antique cars:

1905 Cadillac Runabout Model E	$4,500.00
1910/11 Imperial Touring Model 45	6.500.00
1913 Overland Roadster	2,750.00
1920 Marmon Victoria Touring Model 34	6,250.00
1920 Pierce-Arrow Touring 48 HP	11,000.00
1921 Lincoln V9 Pickup Model L	3,000.00
1921 Velie Touring 5-passenger	3,000.00

1923 child's toy electric auto	$1,200.00
Circa 1925 white park bus	9,000.00
1928 Ford fire truck (pumper) Model AA	3,500.00
1931 Pierce-Arrow Town Sedan Model 41	3,500.00
1928 Rolls-Royce 40–50 h.p. "Phantom I" Sports Tourer	7,840.00
1938 Austin "Cambridge" saloon, used by Sir Winston Churchill while prime minister during World War II	3,780.00

15

By Inheritance

Frequently a deceased owner of antiques and art leaves a will designating one person as executor or possibly two persons as co-executors. This presents real problems, especially to those who have had no experience in settling estates and only a slim knowledge of what is good, or not so good, in the way of personal property.

The U.S. government exempts the net assets of an estate up to a certain figure and then imposes inheritance taxes. State inheritance taxes vary. In our area direct heirs are not taxed but collateral heirs are. It would be as ridiculous to settle an estate without legal advice as it would be to treat a physical ailment without medical advice. So one should immediately retain a reputable attorney. In estates of any size, the Internal Revenue Service also demands, quite properly, that the appraiser of antiques and art be on an approved list or certified as an experienced appraiser.

Once the legal requirements have been satisfied, the question arises as to what to do with the things in the estate. Perhaps a last will directs that everything shall be sold and the proceeds divided. But how to sell the items? They may be sold as a lot to a dealer or they may be given to an auction house or turned over to an individual for a so-called estate sale (each item priced; in some localities this is called a tag sale). Localities and conditions vary. But we do believe that the method of sale is best if it involves some competition among buyers. An experienced dealer buying items as a lot will probably net the estate less than items sold by auction or estate sale would net it, even considering the sales expense involved.

It is difficult to make any hold-fast rule

about the compensation of an appraiser for tax purposes or for the pay to an individual or auction house for selling items by estate sale or auction. But it should be borne in mind that a reputable, experienced appraiser for tax purposes will be fair to both the estate and the government and sometimes save needless argument. In this respect we have found the Internal Revenue Service eminently fair. For tax purposes an appraiser should be entitled to a minimum of $100 a day and expenses. For notable collections, particularly of art, silver, and books and manuscripts, a higher fee may be justified.

In any number of cases a last will and testament designates certain people or institutions to receive specific items of antiques and art. In these cases an executor's task is easy. Once the requirements of the probate or surrogate court and those of the Internal Revenue Service and the state tax commission have been satisfied, those items go without question to the designated persons or institutions. The only possible questions concern items which go to recognized charitable institutions and therefore are exempt from the inheritance taxes.

If all or part of the personal property items are to be sold, then the executor's job is not so easy. Items appraised for tax purposes have been valued on a sort of wholesale or quick-sale basis. This is entirely satisfactory to the Internal Revenue Service, the recognized appraiser having valued on the basis of "what a willing buyer would give a willing seller."

Now come the questions of how to sell items and of the expense involved. Be the sale conducted by an auctioneer or a person offering them in an estate or so-called tag sale, the expense averages about 20 percent of the gross proceeds of the sale. An exception, but not a common one, is the case in which the great auction houses are competing for the sale of a very notable collection and, to get it, are cutting their commission charges. The estate, in any case, is entitled to an amount in excess of the tax appraisal. An ideal situation is when the tax appraisal plus the selling cost of about 20 percent yields the estate approximately the net amount of the tax appraisal. Actually this amount may be more or sometimes less because of various factors and conditions involved.

We feel quite stongly that an executor or administrator, in discussing a possible sale and its probable results, should consult an auctioneer or salesperson who is not a dealer. This eliminates the dealer's temptation to downgrade prices on certain items that he might contemplate buying for resale on his own account. Also a person, or persons, involved should be honest about his own limitations of knowledge. Very few general appraisers or salespeople are experts on books and manuscripts. They should suggest getting information from a real expert in this category, and it would pay the estate to get it. The same holds true of the disposal of Oriental rugs. Antique and semi-antique rugs are in real demand. Asking prices should be made only on the advice of a real expert.

The question of whom an estate representative chooses to conduct a sale depends on what we call "following." Be it an auctioneer, an auction house, a sales organization, or a single salesperson, a "following" is of great importance. A recognized auctioneer or conductor of estate sales advertises a sale and gets crowds because it is generally known that only worthwhile sales are accepted by the advertiser. The public attending the sale more readily pays better prices because of its confidence in whoever is conducting the sale. We cannot overemphasize our belief that the reputation of those conducting a sale is of the utmost importance in the success of any sale of fine antiques and art.

16

To Have & To Hold

The current market in antiques and art is at an all-time high. How come, when the value of our present dollar is estimated in purchasing power at about 60 percent of the 1940 dollar? The poor have always been with us and still are, and it is the hope of all of us that we might do something to alleviate their condition. But those who are what might be called rich and those we simply call successful have incomes that have gone up faster than the value of the dollar has gone down. This has created a surplus of spending money over and above the amount needed for the necessities of everyday living. And a lot of this money is going for the purchase of art and antiques.

To be sure, in England and on the European continent there appears to be less faith in the soundness of currencies, more concern about the price of gold than we have in this country. A by-product of the devaluation of the pound sterling and Britain's continuing economic troubles has been a boom in the antiques and art market. Englishmen who fear more inflation are bidding record sums for furniture, silver, and *objets d'art* at the great auction galleries as a hedge against inflation.

In this country there is much less fear of the future as far as economics are concerned. To be sure, persons having considerable wealth have liked the idea of equity stocks as a guard against inflation. And a few, perhaps, have actually purchased art and antiques with the same thought in mind.

The average successful person in this country realizes that fortunes have been made in the securities markets but also does not forget that fortunes have been lost. To many folks, the buying and selling still seems a little mysterious. When there is extra money to spend, a good antique or an attractive painting is something the whole family can look at, enjoy, and feel that it is not going to slump in value. It is, in other words, a tangible asset. No doubt there are wealthy individuals who get pleasure in going to a safety-deposit box, taking out their portfolios of securities, and admiring the certificates. Ocasionally, of course, when a company has lowered its dividend, the admiration for the stock certificates for that particular concern may not be so great. But tangible assets of grace and beauty do bring lasting everyday pleasure.

About ten years ago the Chase Manhattan Bank started to buy art to hang in the executive quarters and in the public rooms. The total investment is reported to have been about $800,000, and the current market value is about twice that figure.

Mr. Rockefeller's bank is not going to offer this art for sale to realize a profit. But there must be, of course, a satisfaction in knowing that the investment has substantially increased in value. But of far more importance is the thought that this collection of art has afforded real pleasure to those who labor in or do business with this bank.

17

My Own, My Native Land

There are a number of reasons for the increase in interest in (and the prices of) American 19th-century paintings. The astronomical sales prices of the great French Impressionists have almost ruled out all purchasers except museums and millionaires, and art buyers have had to look elsewhere for their acquisitions. This, however, is not the only reason for a turn to 19th-century American paintings. An equally important reason is that they bring us a sense of nostalgia for the past. They depict a country when rivers were for rafts and canoes, undisturbed by roaring outboard motors; when lakes were dotted with sailboats, and no monsters of almost indefinite engine power tried to break the international speed record (or, for all we know, the speed of sound). The skies were peaceful, with no whine of jet engines. The roads were mostly of dirt, and travel along them was by stately carriages or snappy traps, gigs, or buggies drawn by horses. And the most luxurious mode of travel was by Pullman palace car or private railway car.

In the latter part of the 19th century, unlike the Impressionists who had difficulty selling their work, some members of the Hudson School enjoyed popularity and were quite wealthy. Albert Bierstadt, for instance, received as much as $35,000 for a painting. But by the time Frederick Edwin Church, also of the Hudson School, died in 1900, tastes had changed, and he had been almost forgotten. The change and the upsurge in prices have been quite recent. Not so long ago we appraised, for insurance purposes, a delightful work by George Inness entitled *April Showers*. The scene is a beautiful wooded valley, slightly misty because a gentle spring rain is falling. We appraised the painting at $3,500. We wonder what it would bring today.

There is a certain appealing quality in many of these paintings—quiet, peaceful, but altogether human. We think of *The Trapper's Return*, by George Caleb Bingham, a detail of which shows a quiet stream, a funny old wooden canoe with an older bearded man wielding a paddle in the stern, a younger man leaning over a blanket-covered box (no doubt holding the pelts) with his gun crosswise in his arms, and, on a narrow deck forward, a big black cat. Or is it a small black dog? And there is *Country School* by Winslow Homer, a real old-fashioned scene with the schoolmarm wearing a black dress and a white apron covering her skirt and bodice, a crude desk with sawbuck base, and glimpses of three young children. One painter of no particular note we like, perhaps influenced by the fact that he came from our home town of Montpelier, Vermont, is Thomas W. Wood. To us his genre paintings are delightful.

The rise in price of American 19th-century paintings has been dramatic. A Frederick Church went for $3,500 in the early 1950's. Today it would bring $40,000. The price tags on some of his works range from $60,000 to $75,000.

A painting by Thomas Cole was sold recently for $100,000. Five years ago the price would have been about $35,000. In 1950, Coles could be bought for $2,500. A Winslow Homer watercolor went for $10,000 in 1952. Today it would be worth $60,000 to $90,000. Good Homer oils were bringing $4,000 in the 1940's. Just five years ago works by George Caleb Bingham fetched about $25,000. Today they would bring as much as $250,000. Prices of a sizable list of 19th-century painters are steadily rising. The list includes the familiar names of Thomas Eakins, William S. Mount, Albert Bierstadt, William Harnett, George Inness, and Asher B. Durand.

A few years back a dealer friend who was not much up on art, and admitted it, told us a story on himself. In his roaming about he bought five paintings for $50 and put them in his place of business, which was not an art gallery but sort of a storage house for art, antiques, and what have you. A man came in and pointed to one painting. "What are you asking for it?" "What will you give?" "Fifty dollars." "Sold." The painting turned out to be by William Harnett and was worth a pretty penny. The other four paintings held by the dealer were nondescript and worth hardly anything.

18

Don't Tell Anyone!

Just suppose your occupation is such (an independent operator, a professional, or otherwise) that a good-sized part of your income is cash and you know antiques. Even today there are opportunities to buy items that are easily worth the price and in a number of cases will increase in value. So you still make purchases for cash. You possess things that are worthwhile to keep or eventually to sell at a profit, still for cash. And who knows the difference? Purchases of real estate or securities do show up and sometimes arouse suspicion in connection with your tax returns. But you can hardly expect the Internal Revenue Service to enter your house and inquire, "Where did the money come from to buy that antique woven Princess Bokhara rug?" or "How come you have that collection of Burmese glass?" Such operations to avoid income taxes are apparently not too risky and are actually "just peanuts" compared to certain maneuvers with art.

Certain men and women of great wealth collect certain categories of art because they like them and because, in many cases, these purchases give financial encouragement to living artists. Altogether this is very worthwhile, although along the way the art dealers often benefit more than the artists. But there are many so-called "collectors" of art who are using their money power more for capital gains or tax deductions than for any real love for fine paintings.

A work of art acquired at a bargain price can be held for an increase in value and then donated to a museum as a very sizable income-tax deduction: the difference between the original cost and the appraised market value. Also, gifts of art to, say, a lady friend build up her net worth and are not objected to by the tax courts, which have apparently defined such gifts as purely sentimental.

Finally, in estates, an art collection originally costing so much can be liquidated for a tremendous amount more for the purpose of settling inheritance taxes, since death excludes capital gains under tax law. Thus a very sizable hunk of inheritance taxes can be paid off, leaving property that produces revenue for the inheritors.

19

The James Campbell Lewis Sale

The late Mrs. James Campbell Lewis was a friend of ours, a good friend and a useful friend. She purchased a number of important items from estates we were liquidating. She advised us on pricing and how to sell fine items. As a salesperson of good antiques she was the finest strategist we have ever known. For some years she wrote a column for the *Manchester* (New Hampshire) *Union Leader* and very kindly covered the details of estate sales we were conducting.

The first time we saw Mrs. Lewis at her residence, a great house surrounded by many acres along the Connecticut River, she took us out to the greenhouses to show us her collection of geraniums. Being completely ignorant, we thought a geranium was a geranium, not especially beautiful and with a faint, almost disagreeable odor. Mrs. Lewis's geraniums were in different exotic colors and with the delightful smells of roses and other flowers.

Mrs. Lewis's kitchen was a great array of burnished copper pots and pans. Her knowledge of the preparation of good food seemed to be infinite. We do not know if she had ever graduated from the Cordon Bleu. Perhaps she could have given that great institution some lessons.

Mrs. Lewis was born in Budapest and had a fascinating guttural accent. When she telephoned us, there was no necessity of announcing who was calling. There was no mistaking her voice. She was an accomplished horsewoman, and in her younger days in Europe she rode the famous Lippizaner stallions in dressage.

There are some who have the money to make any number of purchases but lack discrimination. Others have real knowledge and insight but lack funds. Mrs. Lewis was a happy combination of taste for what was really good and the money to exercise it. She had a few good art items, but her real interest was in fine antiques: furniture, early silver, glass, porcelain, and jade.

Among the hundreds of items she accumulated were an extensive collection of Canton china and some exceptionally fine semi-antique Oriental rugs.

In her big living room in front of the fireplace Mrs. Lewis had four wing chairs placed at right angles to the fireplace—two facing the other two, with a Queen Anne table between each set of chairs. We wonder how many private residences could have four 18th-century wing chairs and two Queen Anne tea tables "of the period" all in one small group.

After she died, her collection remained almost intact. After Mr. Lewis died, everything was put up at auction. It was good enough and extensive enough that it could be properly catalogued and advertised. Private buyers and dealers seemed to come from everywhere, and the prices paid seemed phenomenal. But the purchasers were considering the quality and rarity of the items.

We would not attempt to list all the hundreds of items in the Lewis auction. But we can list items of great interest and appeal, together with the prices they fetched at the 1971 auction:

Pair of 18th-century brass andirons, American	$400.00
Pair of Queen Anne-style pewter candlesticks	175.00
Queen Anne 18th-century American curly maple tea table	3,500.00
Banjo wall clock by Aaron Willard, Jr.	1,500.00
Silver porringer by Jacob Hurd	2,100.00
American hickory and pine table armchair	6,000.00
American (*circa* 1780) oxbow chest	3,750.00
Old Liverpool jug, "The Boston Pitcher"	475.00
Chinese porcelain table lamp	375.00
Six matching American Queen Anne side chairs	30,000.00
American Queen Anne cherry desk on lowboy	6,000.00
American 18th-century courting mirror, all original	700.00
American Windsor brace back side chair with fine turnings	600.00
18th-century Massachusetts block-front chest	4,500.00

Mahogany fall-front serpentine desk attributed to Benjamin Frothingham	$4,750.00
American Windsor comb-back armchair with knuckle arms	1,500.00
George III London silver coffee pot by John Scofield	575.00
American William and Mary highboy	2,750.00
American Hepplewhite Pembroke table	1,250.00
Terry shelf clock, electrified	400.00
18th-century American Queen Anne stool	2,500.00
Silver can by John Ball, Concord, Mass.	1,600.00
Wooden cannonball carrier used as an umbrella stand	225.00
18th-century block-front highboy attributed to Townsend	42,500.00
American Hepplewhite sideboard	4,350.00
Pair of early Delft tobacco jars	1,000.00
Silver castor by John Burt	2,100.00
Brace-back fanback Windsor side chair	600.00
Pine corner cabinet	4,000.00
American maple oblong table, sunken top, scroll apron, plain pad feet	4,000.00
Rare Goddard chest on desk, block front base	60,000.00
Duncan Phyfe drop-leaf pedestal library table	1,800.00
Duncan Phyfe settee with two matching armchairs (of interest to us because we sold these items to Mrs. Lewis in the early 1950's)	3,000.00